Success & Something Greater

YOUR MAGIC KEY

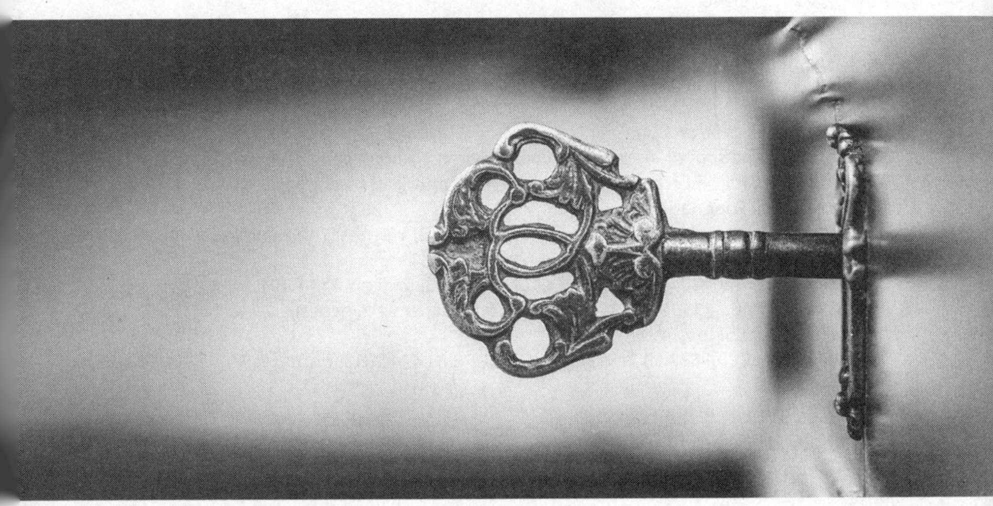

By Sharon Lechter & Dr. Greg Reid

Published and Distributed by
SOUND WISDOM
PO Box 310
Shippensburg, PA 17257-0310
717-530-2122

info@soundwisdom.com

www.soundwisdom.com

Cover/Jacket designer

ISBN 13 TP: 978-1-64095-075-7

ISBN 13 eBook: 978-1-64095-074-0

Library of Congress Cataloging-in-Publication Data

Names: Lechter, Sharon L., author. | Reid, Greg S., author.
Title: Success and something greater : your magic key where ideas become
   realities / by Sharon Lechter and Greg S. Reid ; authorized by The
   Napoleon Hill Foundation.
Description: Shippensburg, PA : Sound Wisdom, [2018] | Series: Think and grow
   rich series | Includes bibliographical references and index.
Identifiers: LCCN 2018043804 (print) | LCCN 2018045251 (ebook) | ISBN
   9781640950740 | ISBN 9781640950733 (trade paper : alk. paper)
Subjects: LCSH: Success. | New Thought.
Classification: LCC BF637.S8 (ebook) | LCC BF637.S8 L424 2018 (print) | DDC
   158--dc23
LC record available at https://lccn.loc.gov/2018043804

For Worldwide Distribution, Printed in the U.S.A.

1 2 3 4 5 6 / 21 20 19

Since the dawn of man, it has been our
deepest instinct to seek meaning.

With each generation growing more
impatient, we desire information and
answers at lightning speed.

In your hands are the digestible nuggets of
wisdom distilled from today's top minds.

Each modern leader was asked to explain
their secret to living a life of sustained
abundance, whether it be personal,
business, or otherwise.

We had a single mission: When unlocking
the door to success, share with us…

What is your magic key?

The subconscious mind may be
likened to a magnet, and when
it has been vitalized and thoroughly
saturated with any

DEFINITE PURPOSE

it has a decided tendency to
atttract all that is necessary for
the fulfillment of that purpose.

—Napoleon Hill

The Great Magic Key to Success

This contains excerpts from a Truthful Advertising article Napoleon Hill developed in 1917.

In presenting to you this Great Magic Key, let me first explain that it is no invention of mine.

This Great Magic Key is the most wonderful power, yet perfectly simple in operation. So simple that most people have failed to make use of it. We human beings are too prone to look askance at so simple a formula for success—a formula which will open the door to health and wealth; yet such a formula is the Great Magic Key.

It will unlock the door to riches! It will unlock the door to fame! And, in many cases it will unlock the door to physical health. It will unlock the door to education. It will let you into the storehouse of all your latent ability. It will act as a pass-key to almost any position in your life you may choose.

Through the Great Magic Key we have unlocked the secret doors to all of the world's great inventions. Through its magic powers all of our great geniuses have been produced.

You are a laborer, in a menial position, and desire a better position in life. The Great Magic Key will help you attain it! Through its use, Carnegie, Rockefeller, Hill, Harriman, Morgan and Guggenheim have accumulated millions of dollars in material wealth.

You ask—"What is this Great Magic Key?"

And I answer with one word: Concentration!

Now let me define "concentration" in the sense that it is here mentioned. First, I wish it to be clearly understood that I have no reference to anything occult or mysterious. Concentration, as the term is here used, does not mean sitting in a room with your eyes steadfastly fixed on a knot-hole!

It means, in the sense that I am using it, the ability, through fixed habit and practice, of keeping your mind on one subject until you have thoroughly familiarized yourself with that subject and mastered it!

Stating it in another way, it means the ability to THINK—the ability to organize knowledge that you acquire from all sources concerning a given subject—the ability to use that knowledge in a practical manner.

In concentrating on any subject, you must THINK. Remember that mind wandering is not THINKING! Efficient, scientific thinking contemplates the ability to direct your mind up and down the various limbs of the tree that represents the subject of your thought, following each limb to the end and retracing it back to the trunk of the tree, but keeping the mind always on the tree as a whole. Various counter-attractions will lead your mind away from the tree of your subject, but you must learn to bring it back to the original subject before it wanders too far. This ability is concentration!

To stop here would be insufficient. You must know more concerning the use of this Great Magic Key! First, let me tell you that Ambition and Desire are the great dynamic powers which you must summon to the aid of Concentration. Without ambition and desire the Great Magic Key is useless. That is why so few people use the Key.

Desire whatever you may, and if your desire is strong enough the Great Magic Key of Concentration will help you attain it, if the object of your desire is something which is humanly possible to attain.

See yourself as a person of influence in the business world. See yourself increasing in value and earning still more money as you grow older. See yourself engaged in a line of work where you will not fear the loss of a job. Paint this picture through the powers of your imagination, and lo! it will turn into a beautiful picture of Desire. Use this Desire as the chief object of your Concentration and see what happens!

You now have the secret of the Great Magic Key! It will unlock the door to whatever position in life you want, if that position is humanly possible of attainment. It will make of you a better citizen if the object of your concentration is a worthy one. Do not underestimate the value of the Great Magic Key because it is not clothed with mysticism, or because it is written in simple language that anyone may easily understand. All great truths are simple in the final analysis.

Use this Great Key with intelligence! Use it only for the attainment of worthy purpose and it will give you the things of life for which your heart may crave. So simple, so easy of application, yet so marvelous in results! Try it! Begin all over again and make the next five or ten years tell a story of human accomplishment in whatever line of work your calling may have placed you, that you will not be ashamed of—that the generations of your family yet to come will be proud of!

Make a name for yourself through—Ambition, Desire, and Concentration!

—Napoleon Hill

Napoleon Hill's explanation of the Magic Key, the power of concentration combined with ambition and desire, while written decades ago, still holds very true today. How concentration, ambition and desire are combined, however, can take many different forms.

When we decided to write *Success and Something Greater: Your Magic Key*, we wanted to interview successful people in various industries and walks of life to discover some of these applications. You will discover the magic keys they used in creating their success.

Challenge yourself to learn from each of their stories, and apply their wisdom to refine and accelerate your own Magic Key to Success.

—Sharon Lechter and Greg Reid

Table of Contents

Chapter One

Thoughts Become Things

*You feel what you think; you think what
you feel—automatically.*

In *Think and Grow Rich*, Napoleon Hill used the phrase "thoughts are things." We can claim ownership of our thoughts and credit for the actions we take in conjunction with them. However, by itself, is a thought sufficient to produce our desired level of results and success?

The answer, according to Hill, is no. While thoughts are things, their ability to produce a desired outcome is dependent on the emotion, or feeling, that accompanies that thought. Emotions have a tremendous impact on our thoughts, and depending on the emotion and whether it is positive or negative, each thought could be an asset or a deficit to our progress. It is also true that the greater the level of feeling that accompanies each thought, the more likely it is that we will actually act on it.

You feel what you think—you think what you feel. Let's decipher that statement. We all have thoughts, either positive, negative, or indifferent. Those thoughts will produce correlating feelings. When we think negative thoughts, we will have bad feelings. When our thoughts are positive, they will likewise produce good feelings.

But according to the phrase, we also think what we feel. In other words, our emotions influence the thoughts we have. It's something we've all experienced—when we're happy or excited, the thoughts generated are typically very positive. Feelings and thoughts, therefore, can be construed to be inseparable.

As Hill states, when thoughts are paired with emotions, they will have the most impact on our success. It's a thought-provoking philosophy that deserves further consideration.

John Assaraf is an interesting case study. In his early years, he was considered what people might call a hustler. He would do just about anything and everything to get what he wanted. Young John cheated on school exams, stole, got in frequent fights, and struggled to learn. In fact, in his first *New York Times* bestselling book, *Having It All,* he is affectionately known as "The Street Kid." He was the stereotype of the kid least likely to succeed.

To the surprise of his parents and teachers, John turned his life around. The principles he employed and learned helped him build five multimillion-dollar companies in real estate, Internet software, business coaching and consulting, and brain research. Currently, he is the founder of Praxis Now, a company that develops brain-training products that drive individuals to achieve excellence using the latest evidence-based neural science. He does this by using a proprietary blend of technology and support so that people and corporations may achieve quantum learning.

Given his expertise in the complexities of the brain, John was a perfect source for learning more about Hill's philosophy.

We sat down with John, and he offered insights that differed in important ways from conventional thinking.

A long-time fan and advocate of *Think and Grow Rich*, John relates that while the late Dr. Hill claimed that "thoughts are things," there is another perspective that deserves equal consideration. In John's own words, "Thoughts, *over time*, become things."

Over the past several years, new brain discoveries have proven this concept to be true, albeit with a twist.

Over time, thoughts create patterns, which, in turn, become beliefs.

These beliefs drive our perceptions and behaviors.

The fact is that the more we repeat a pattern, the easier it will become for our mind to recall and act upon it. Dr. Hill also addressed this principle, stating that "any impulse of thought which is repeatedly passed on to the subconscious mind is, finally, accepted and acted upon by the subconscious mind, which proceeds to translate that impulse into its physical equivalent, by the most practical procedure available."

In other words, the more frequently a thought is repeated, the more likely it is that the subconscious mind will act upon it and produce a result—a thing. This is more than a theory. As John explains, there is scientific support to this claim.

"Thoughts are simply electric currents in the brain, and for the first time we can map what's happening inside the brain—thus we know that thoughts DO matter."

John states that as soon as you've learned something and set a new pattern, it takes 56 days for that pattern to be reinforced and to sink in. This becomes your new thought.

What's shocking, though, is that it is much faster to trigger a painful thought than a positive one. It's also been proven that it takes three to five positive thoughts to counter a single negative one. That means that negative thoughts are more powerful and have more influence on our subconscious mind than positive thoughts. As a result, we have to be more cognizant of our thoughts and make an intentional effort to create positive thoughts to produce positive things in our lives.

Once negative thoughts are set in motion, the only way to change them is to deploy what is referred to as a pattern interruption, diverting our attention from a negative or painful thought to a positive one.

For example, when a child falls and scrapes his arm, it will hurt, and he'll start to cry.

Rather than focusing on the situation that occurred, we could ask, "Hey, are those new shoes?" pointing down from the injury and focusing his attention on his feet.

The moment the child looks down and notices his sneakers, his mind shifts from the accident to his new kicks. Instantly, he is drawn away from the circumstance and will stop crying, thus forming a pattern interruption that causes him to begin to forget what just happened.

John Assaraf explains this principle as follows: "The thoughts we have on an ongoing basis develop the patterns in the brain. The patterns in the brain that we think about the most lower the firing threshold in that pattern. That simply means that it makes it easier for us to think about that which we think about most. And it gives us the ability to focus more on what we think about most. The key question is, are you thinking about what you want most of the time, or are you thinking about what you don't want most of the time?"

We emotionalize what we do think about and either take action or don't take action on it, depending on how it feels. The more we think about a particular thing, the more likely it is that we will act upon it. And, as Dr. Hill stated decades ago, the more emotion we give to that thought, the greater the probability that the thought will come to fruition and manifest itself in our lives.

The reverse of this is called RAS, which is also known as the Reticular Activating System. John Assaraf defines the RAS in more technical terms, stating that it comes from the thalamus gland, a filtration system in the brain that processes everything we see, smell, hear, taste, and touch and determines if we will focus on it or not.

In layman's terms, the RAS draws one's attention toward what one focuses on. If you're thinking about what you want, your brain will notice more of it. If you're thinking about what you don't want, the brain will also seek those things. Simply put, your brain will always seek precisely what it is that you focus your attention on. It happens every day, and most often we aren't even aware of it.

How many times have you purchased a new car and then suddenly you start seeing the same exact vehicle everywhere you go? You pull out of the dealership in the shiny red sports car you've been wanting for years, and as you're driving down the freeway there are shiny red sports cars everywhere you look. Suddenly, it seems like everybody owns a shiny red sports car! Is this a coincidence? No. Those cars were always there, yet you simply didn't notice them until you had a reason to do so. This is the Reticular Activating System at work, noticing more of the things you want or have.

Therefore, this philosophy works both ways—your brain searches and finds both the things you already have and the things you desire. What if you have a desire to include an animal in your family? For example, let's say you've done your research and have decided that a Collie is the best fit and you want a pup, a dog that you can train and acclimate to the family at a young age. However, in hindsight, you haven't heard about a single Collie being available, let alone a pup. Suddenly by chance, a friend tells you about a relative who has Collie pups that will be available soon...only to be followed by ads and co-workers who, seemingly out of the blue, mention that they, too, know where you can find a puppy.

This is the same philosophy that gave birth to the saying "When the student is ready, the teacher will appear." In other words, there is always someone who can and will teach us those things we want to learn; however, we didn't notice their presence until we were ready to learn and were looking for them. Until we choose to seek, we will not find.

For example, let's say you're interested in becoming a chef. The thought, and the desire, are in your mind, but you aren't aware of any culinary institutions nearby and haven't heard of any for months. As you begin to seek a culinary instructor, though, you are suddenly fed with leads via e-mail, the Internet, and the people with whom you talk. Now you have not only obtained leads, but you also have choices. When the student is ready, the teacher will appear.

Let's expound on this theory and take it to another level by applying it to opportunities. Imagine that you are looking for a job or a business opportunity. Initially, the prospects appear dim. The economy is struggling, and everyone you know has had difficulty finding a new job. You try but don't have any confidence that anything will present itself in the very near future. However, the thought and the desire exist. Suddenly, even when you are not consciously seeking those opportunities, they begin to appear, and you not only have an opportunity, but you find that you have multiple opportunities from which to select. Even when you weren't actively looking for them, the thought, the seed, was planted in your brain, and it went to work to produce the physical reality of your thoughts.

In reality, our minds are always actively looking for things, people, and situations that match what we are thinking about in an effort to align with the chemical/electrical state within ourselves. We will only find and see that which matches with what is in our brain.

If we are happy, our mind will seek things that will bring us more happiness.

If we are angry, it will be sure to find more things that will make us even angrier. As a result, we in essence become addicted to our emotional state, even if we don't like it. The more we repeat a pattern, whether it is good or bad, happy or sad, the more addicted we become to that emotional state. Then the brain looks for the exact person, place, or situation that matches the chemical state to which it has become accustomed.

A simple way to illustrate this process is by imagining a radio receiver in your car, home, or office. Logic would tell us that music is running through the airwaves at all times. There is country, rock, rap, hip-hop, and even a little R&B circulating through the airwaves. Once we TUNE into the frequency we desire, we pull from the ethers what we are seeking and in the mood for at the time, and instantly it is delivered.

Now think of your mind as that receiver. What is it tuned into?

Whether it's romance, a business transaction, wealth, fame, sadness, health, sickness, or anger, your brain will seek and find more of the same. Whatever we tune into and vibrate with is what we attract and invite into our lives. The more we tune into it, the more we will seek and find it—positive or negative, the brain does not differentiate. This explains why some people may seem to have only good or bad luck. It is also why one person might always seem to be in a state of drama, while another person might always be in a state of abundant cash flow. One may be the hit of every party and gathering, where another may find trouble no matter where they find themselves. Virtually every circumstance in our life can be attributed to this philosophy.

What happens when we're stuck in a poverty mindset, drama, or negativity? We are actually in a process called repetition compulsion, where we are compelled to repeat patterns over and over again. Again, the thoughts in our brain will create similar results in our life, even if they are not the results we would prefer. Because our thoughts over time become things, the only way to reverse or change the results is to change our thoughts. If we're stuck in a negative cycle, we need to interrupt the pattern of our thoughts, stopping the negative and replacing it with a positive alternative. To have something different, we must break the undesired loop and replace it with something that we do want or that inspires us.

To do this, John Assaraf suggests that we implement what he calls the 4R Pattern Interruption System.

1. **Recognition (awareness):** Before we can change a thought or pattern, we must become aware of our current thoughts. What are your thought patterns, and are they moving you away from or toward your goals?

2. **Reframe (thought pattern interruption):** Once you become aware of a particular thought pattern, you can change it by diverting your attention—or in this case, your thoughts—to something else. Another way to accomplish this task is to reframe the meaning of what is causing the thought pattern. You can add a couple words to an existing thought or pattern to reframe it. For example, saying, "I'm always sad" is a pattern. Simply adding a couple words to that thought reframes it, and the thought becomes, "I'm always sad, but I choose to be happy."

3. **Release (let go of patterns that do not serve you):** Make a decision to rise above the thought/emotion. The thought patterns we establish over the years become habits; however, they are often based on old thoughts and emotions that no longer serve us. Recognizing them and letting them go is within our power. Only then can we replace them with patterns that are aligned with the things we currently want.

Thoughts become things. Dr. Hill said this best. The only thing we have control over is our thoughts.

4. **Retrain (reprogram the brain to have a new pattern):** Because thoughts become patterns that we habitually repeat, we have to make a conscious, intentional effort to retrain the brain with a new pattern. By taking small steps every day, you can develop a different pattern. Therefore, small and repeated incremental strides will be necessary to retrain the brain to focus on that which we want to attract.

FRACTIONAL STEPS

Like the old saying goes, "How do you eat a whale? One bite at a time." Our thought patterns weren't created overnight. They took months, maybe even years, to form, and it will, of course, take time to change them. The first step, though, is to become aware of what you want and recognize whether your thoughts are aligned toward...or away from...that desire. Over time, your thoughts will produce results. If you don't like the results you're getting, you must first change your thoughts.

*The key to making any improvement lies
in the willingness to take action.*

As has been quoted frequently, the journey of a thousand miles begins with a single step. Often, it's the most important step we'll ever make. Like thoughts, that step repeated over time will produce the desired results. But you'll remain stuck in the cycle you're in if you don't take that first step.

Sure, it takes time—most things worthwhile in life take time and attention. Remember, it took many days for your current thoughts to sink in and become a habit. Understandably, it will require a similar investment of time to create a new thought pattern. Like John Assaraf stated, the key is to engage in small, incremental, and repetitious steps to make that change occur.

When we talked to John, we asked him to provide a blueprint that would help people implement the Four Rs as quickly as possible. He provided a simplified step-by-step process we all can follow:

"You can get better at anything by recognizing where you currently are. What level are you at in a particular area of your life, whether it is health, wealth, business, academics, or any other venture?" First and foremost, recognize where you are, what John refers to as your "true north." "Then, reframe your brain around how to get to the next level by focusing on that and releasing the thoughts, emotions, and behaviors that have kept you at the level where you are. The next step is to retrain the brain around the thoughts, habits, emotions, and behaviors of the next level."

Sometimes, we don't get to that point because we accept where we are, becoming complacent with our lives as they are. According to Dr. Hill, this could be the result of becoming accustomed to where we are and the emotions or feelings with which we become comfortable over time. Dr. Hill likened this to the way people grow to accept criminal behaviors, using the words of a famous criminologist: "When men first come into contact with crime, they abhor it. If they remain in contact with crime for a time, they become accustomed to it, and endure it. If they remain in contact with it long enough, they finally embrace it, and become influenced by it."

John Assaraf took this explanation a degree further, stating that the key factor in whether we take the steps necessary to create changes lies in whether we are interested in or committed to what we want. There is a difference. "If you are committed, you will do whatever it takes—and there are different levels of commitment. The challenge is to make the changes necessary to achieve our new goal. Like a thermostat in a room, our brain keeps us in our comfort zone. To get out of that comfort zone, we have to reset the thermostat and increase our level of comfort." According to John, that can be accomplished in small steps, taking just five minutes a day. In other words, the effort does not have to be monumental, but over time, with the implementation and repetition of new thoughts every day, the results can be.

This is true for everything we focus on, from wealth to health. John went on to explain the role thoughts play in our brain: "Every time we have a thought, an electrical signal is sent. Every cell in the body feels that electrical signal. There is a chemical that is released in the body. If you're thinking about being sick and unhealthy or out of shape, you are recreating more of the same. We need to be very aware that our thoughts make a huge difference.

"When you think about what you feel, and you feel what you think about, you will set up a pattern for that thought and/or feeling. Anything you do repetitiously becomes a pattern over time. Are you reaffirming what you don't want, or can you transcend that pattern, think about what you do want, and take one step toward that? From there, it's just a matter of becoming aware of that thought pattern and switching it."

We need to be cognizant of our thoughts and the feelings we have around them all of the time. That's because the things we want continually change. At one stage of life, we might be more success or family oriented, while another stage finds us becoming more health oriented. Therefore, the awareness of what we want plays a crucial role in our thoughts and the outcomes produced by them.

From the time John was in his early 20s, he has used his mind to create the life that he wants. His thoughts have become things as he created patterns that brought him success in several industries and increased his expertise in how the brain works and how we respond to the thoughts we feed it.

Through the teachings of Dr. Hill and experts like John Assaraf, we can begin to view the brain as more than a vessel of learning that stores knowledge. The philosophies of these two instrumental thought leaders and the scientific research that supports them prove that the brain not only has the power to receive thought, but it also has the ability to act automatically on that thought without action or direction on our part. It will happen with or without our participation. The one and only power we hold in this process is the ability to control which thoughts we feed our brain. When we accomplish that feat, we can direct our brain to produce more of the things we do want and less of the things we do not want.

John Assaraf supports and reinforces the teachings that Napoleon Hill shared with us in 1937. He has used those teachings to create multiple successes and has been steadfast and instrumental in the research that supports these theories. Today, John uses his philosophy to create even more fulfillment in his life by spending time with the people and things that bring him joy.

John's new mantra is *"Do MORE of what you love, LESS of what you tolerate, and NONE of what you hate."*

To accomplish that goal, John is applying what he is teaching us today and focusing on what drives him in a positive light. It's a philosophy that's deserving of significant thought, and John knows when he pairs thought with emotion, over time, his thought—his goal—will evolve into what he wants. He has taken the first step and planted the seed of thought in his mind. By watering it daily and being attentive to it, it will grow to fruition.

*** Thoughts become things…what
are you thinking?***

Chapter Two

Find Your True Purpose and Set a Goal

Know your true purpose and set a goal—
it will move you to action.

If it is true that your thoughts become "things" over time, it is also true that those "things" will continuously influence your daily life. Harnessing the power of your thoughts is much easier when you know your true purpose. It will allow you to focus your thoughts on achieving that purpose through setting specific and strategic goals. Another philosophy states that if you have a goal, it will move you to action. By creating the goal, you are identifying that goal as a "thing," as something tangible that you can make happen simply by stating the goal into existence.

Throughout this chapter, we are going to focus on the idea that where you put your focus is where your day will go and, over time, where your life will go. If you choose to identify your purpose and set goals and then remain true in your efforts to meet those goals, you will have the opportunity to watch the life you want unfold before your eyes.

There is a parable about an old man who has been a beggar his entire life. He spends his days sitting on a small, old oak box by the side of the road, waiting for strangers to come by so he can gain pity and then, hopefully, money. The old beggar has traveled the countryside for as long as he can remember with only a few possessions—his loyal dog and his small box to sit on—in search of spare change and food scraps. He found himself on the side of the road in another nameless small town, again hungry, tired, and disenchanted with the world.

As another stranger was passing by, the beggar held out his hand and gave his usual time-tested but dispirited request for spare change. "Spare a few coins?" the beggar tiredly asked. The stranger stopped in front of the old man and looked him up and down. Rather than offer spare change, the man said, "I might have a dollar or two, but what's in the box?" pointing to the old but interesting wooden box on which the beggar was sitting. Surprised by getting a question rather than a few coins, the old beggar replied, "There's nothing in this old box, stranger. I just use it to keep a few inches off the ground when I sit, and I've carried it forever. How about that dollar?"

The stranger did not move, but once again pointed to the old oak box and asked the old man, "What is inside your box?" this time a bit louder and with more force than before. The beggar began to get agitated and reiterated to the stranger that "There's nothing inside the box, and if you have nothing to give, perhaps you should just move along." The stranger, once again unmoved by the beggar's response, told the old man, "You must look in the box, or I'll just have to ask again." "Fine," responded the beggar, figuring the only way he might get rid of this man is to just look inside the box to show the man that it is, in fact, empty as he had stated.

He picked his tired body off his wooden perch and fumbled with a rusty old iron clasp. The clasp gave way with the smack of a rock, and the beggar pulled on the lid as the hinges creaked. As the lid finally opened with a thud and the sunlight shined in, he was astonished to find that the small old box was full of gold and silver. Everything the beggar ever needed was there inside that box the whole time and had been with him through each struggle. Each time the old man had to beg for food or sleep outside, the gold had been with him.

You'll soon learn the same is true for you, your life, and what you need to live a life of abundance. Every last thing you need to create the life you want lives inside of you. Just like the old beggar with his box of gold, you possess all the tools necessary to create success, happiness, and a life of purpose. We live in a world so full of noise and distractions. One of the most difficult tasks ahead of you is to become the master of your mind, to learn to quiet the noise and tune into that gold instead. That's where the magic lies—your passion, your purpose, and your dreams exist in that place inside of you. In order to access it, you must simply tune in. Just as John Assaraf explained to us in chapter 1, your mind is the receiver and you have to be aware of what exactly you are tuning into.

What is your true purpose? Only when you know this can you set goals to accomplish it. Setting your goal is the beginning of the process, but it isn't enough just to have set your goal. Setting your goal isn't the finish line. This is where everything is just getting started. Setting the goal is your beginning, the starting point for something amazing. Once you commit to your goal, there's a magic something that breathes it to life. There is something more that goes along with your goal, acting in unison with it, helping to bring to life something you created with your thoughts. That something is faith, and it works around the clock to help move you toward the life of your dreams.

Napoleon Hill talked about faith as if it were a palpable thing you could reach out and grab—something so definitive, so real, and so important that he made it a part of his success formula and wrote about it substantially in *Think and Grow Rich*. Dr. Hill so appropriately said, "Faith is the eternal elixir which gives life, power, and action to the impulse of thought!"

The person who believes in their purpose so much that they are able to apply that faith and use that faith will turn their thoughts into reality. They accomplish what seems to onlookers to be a miracle. They turn their thoughts into things. The person who reaches out and grasps the prize, propelled purely by their belief in their purpose and their vision, is an alchemist by turning their thoughts (base metal) into things (gold). With the magnitude of their faith they can accomplish anything... And so can you, by practicing the same principles. Faith breathes life into the impulse of thought, giving power to something that did not exist until you took the time to become aware of it and actively think it into existence.

The amazing thing about faith is that it is free to obtain and, once obtained, that faith can grow as large as you will allow it to grow. You are exactly who you are because of the thoughts you allow to dominate and occupy your mind. Your thoughts determine your goals. Your faith, combined with those goals, determines your outcome. By taking control of your thoughts, applying faith to them, and then taking action, you become the master of your life. You begin to live your life deliberately. You fulfill your purpose.

Let us tell you about Lisa Copeland, a woman who is a fabulous example of living life on purpose. A woman in a male-dominated industry, Lisa was instrumental in bringing the FIAT brand back to the United States. With more than 25 years of success, she is a pioneer in the field of automotive sales and brand strategy. In 2015, *Automotive News* named her among the Top 100 Women in the Automotive Industry. Through her trailblazing past, Lisa empowers women to pursue their own success, and in doing so, she fulfills her own purpose.

After selling her award-winning automobile dealership in 2016, Lisa has been pursuing her passion and purpose to lead others who are committed to transforming businesses, building world-class organizations, and working with management and sales teams. "Fear LESS" and "Keep crushing it" are the mottos by which she lives and works. When we asked Lisa what the "it" is in "Keep crushing it," she told us that it is one thing that holds people and businesses back: mediocrity.

"Mediocre people around you can hold your business back. People accept the status quo and are not willing to hold themselves to a higher level. Your legacy is your end-of-life story. The majority of people accept what has happened to them in the past, instead of trying to rewrite their legacy."

Lisa has written an impressive legacy. As the creator of Buying-CarsHerWay.com, she is committed to empowering women consumers. In 2012, the Girl Scouts Central Texas named her a "Woman of Distinction." In the same year, the *Austin Business Journal* named her one of the "Five Most Powerful Women in Austin." As a woman in a male-dominated field, Copeland and her team became the first FIAT retailer to break the NAFTA sales record by selling more than 100 new FIAT 500s in one month. That impressive record earned Lisa and her team a visit by Fiat Chrysler Automobiles (FCA) Chairman Sergio Marchionne, as well as the FCA's highest honor: the Walter P. Chrysler Award for sales and service excellence. But this remarkable achievement did not happen by accident. Lisa set a goal and deliberately took action with her team to break the record.

Mr. Marchionne was Lisa's automotive and business hero. After she heard him make a speech in 2010 at the Orlando Dealer Announcement Show named "A Promise for a Promise," Lisa knew she wanted an automotive career that would not only have sales success but would leave a forever footprint on the industry. Mr. Marchionne saved the Chrysler Corporation from disaster by living the philosophy "a promise for a promise" every day. Simple, straightforward, uncomplicated. A business philosophy that believes everybody wins, everybody is responsible. Those are the words that drove Lisa daily. Mr. Marchionne passed away on July 24, 2018, after a short illness, but his legacy lives on through Lisa and the entire automotive industry.

Lisa's outstanding career would make anyone take notice, but we found her achievements to be even more impressive because she broke the proverbial glass ceiling that many women have encountered but have not been able to crack.

"The boys' club has tried to freeze women, minorities, and millennials in the land of trucks and SUVs. We broke the previous sales record because everybody loved our story and rooted for us," Lisa explained.

Lisa reminded us that she didn't do this alone; she credits the fact that she intentionally surrounds herself with people who are at a higher level—people who aren't willing to settle for being average.

"All people struggle with mediocrity," she said. "Mediocrity lives within men and women. You have to make a conscious decision to pull out of it."

We asked Lisa to tell us the keys to crushing mediocrity. That is when she shared her success equation:

$$P + P = P$$

People + Purpose = Profit

"Once you have the right people and the right purpose, profit will come. People have a purpose to make money, but that will never withstand the long haul," she explained. "Once you have an organization with a higher purpose, you are able to attract like-minded people who know who is supposed to be on the train with you...or who isn't. They buy into your purpose."

It made sense, but we were curious how one comes to their purpose...and finds the right people to support it. She told us it's by simply asking, and honestly answering, a few questions:

- What is your "higher" purpose?

- Who do you want to be?

- With what kind of people do you want to surround yourself?

"It takes a lot of soul searching to find your true purpose. You have to try a lot of different things," Lisa told us. "One question that I ask the audience when I speak is, 'Do you think what you do matters?'"

She went on to explain that every job matters but not everyone feels that what they do really matters. "The person taping the box to ship it in commerce is just as important as the person who opens the box. What you do matters; and if you don't feel it does, you have to do something different."

According to Lisa, those who don't believe what they do matters are those who live in mediocrity. They don't give it their all because they are not working toward their purpose. Giving it your all is critical to success.

"My young sales team broke the world record. We were selling a micro car in Texas, a land of trucks and SUVs. We were told it couldn't be done. Nobody else had said out loud that they wanted to break a world sales record. But I did; I even made a bet with the press that we would!"

With a goal to meet Sergio Marchionne, the most powerful person in the automotive industry, Lisa told her team that breaking the world record and meeting Mr. Marchionne would change their lives and careers. The other sales teams in the FCA Group were mediocre, but Lisa's team wasn't. They were motivated and driven by their goal.

"When the chairman of the board flew in on a Gulfstream jet, he was dumbfounded. That is when I saw a young team do the same thing the good old boys could do in this industry. Not only did we do it, but we kicked their butts! Our entire industry was mired in mediocrity, and we broke it," said Lisa.

She credits this ability to crush mediocrity with having a purpose. "All of the successful people I have done business with know their purpose. They know why they are doing what they're doing, and they believe it matters. Those who don't seem to flounder. They have mild success, but they don't have record-breaking success."

Today, Lisa Copeland continues to crush mediocrity. She shares her message of overcoming fear and rising above mediocrity in her book *Crushing Mediocrity*, co-authored by her co-founder of the Crushing It Academy, René Banglesdorf, the CEO of Charlie Bravo Aviation. An international keynote speaker and award-winning sales strategist, Lisa follows her purpose, knowing that what she does really matters. In addition to sharing her own message, Lisa is a great advocate of Napoleon Hill's work and has endorsed and promoted the message of empowering women in the book *Think and Grow Rich for Women* and the message of how to overcome your fear in the book *Outwitting the Devil*.

Doing enough is never enough. Being enough is never enough. Success requires a higher level of action, drive, and commitment. Put your fears aside and dare to do what others believe cannot be done. If you believe what you're doing matters and surround yourself with the right people who buy into your purpose and goal, you too can rewrite your legacy.

The average person will get average results. To get to the top, you've got to keep mediocrity from holding you back. Keep on crushing it.

The saying "easier said than done" definitely applies here. For each time we try, there will be at least one subsequent failure or setback. The process of setting goals and achieving them is not an easy feat. If it were, everyone would be wildly successful, living their purpose daily, and conquering the world with their morning coffee. Early on, identifying the amount of effort you are willing to put in will be paramount to your success. Recognizing the need for daily effort before you start will allow you to create a more realistic approach to your goals. Once again, what we are talking about here is mastering your thoughts.

One of the most powerful things you have access to is your thoughts. Your most powerful agent for change isn't outside of yourself. We often falsely believe a boss or a résumé holds the key to our fate, but the truth is that the key to fate, progress, and growth is nestled in the power of the thoughts you think. Just like the old beggar who discovered everything he ever needed once he opened his box of gold, the same will be true once you open your mind and begin to master your thoughts. You don't need to waste any more of your precious time looking outward for the answers that already exist inside of you.

If you knew the true power of your thoughts, you would pay much more attention to where you direct your focus day in and day out. Your thoughts are running a continuous cycle through your mind every microsecond of every day, shaping your reality. It is much easier to learn to tune them out over choosing to tune into these thoughts. The path of least resistance is the one that requires less effort and, in this case, tuning out is much easier. More often than not, we find ourselves ignoring the thoughts that have taken hold in our minds, so we end up on the path of least resistance.

Given the busyness of the world in which we live and the constant noise, most of us need daily reminders to drive deliberate action. This helps us to keep our focus where it needs to be. Otherwise, by default, we all end up off track, tuning out our powerful and important thoughts without making progress toward our dreams. When we allow our minds to become clouded with all the things and thoughts that don't matter, our life becomes one that doesn't matter, even to us, as by not taking deliberate action, we meander down a path leading nowhere. Lisa was clear about her goal, was focused on achieving it, had faith it could be done and that it supported her purpose, and took the steps to empower her team to ultimately break the world sales record.

By being deliberate in your thoughts, you are allowing yourself to remain active in the pursuit of your dreams and your purpose. You take a step backward every day that you focus on doubt that allows you to dream up creative excuses for not achieving your goals. You have to believe in what you are doing or what you are going to do. The universe exists to provide you with what you seek. If you constantly focus on doubt, if all of your energy funnels into feeding your doubt, then the universe synchronizes with your doubt and delivers even more doubt.

You are delivered what you order in our attraction-based universe. Imagine going to the Four Seasons and telling the sommelier that you don't want Merlot, that you don't want Pinot Noir, and that you don't like wines from the Var region of France. You point out that you don't care for semi-sweet wines, and you really have a strong distaste for anything too dry. How could they possibly bring you a bottle of anything you would enjoy, when all you've shared with them is what you don't want? It's the same with the universe. If you dwell on doubt, you are only ordering up more doubt. The universe aligns with your thoughts and delivers a perfect match to your specific focus.

The world around you—the world you see and exist within—is a direct reflection of your own thoughts and your daily focus. Focus on positivity, and you will find yourself enjoying a positive existence. Focus on negativity, and you will find yourself confused as to why your life is so bad. Your reality always mirrors the thoughts on which you focus.

Imagine you are ready for a new partner. You have been feeling very alone lately, and you don't want to be alone anymore. But you spend most of your time thinking about being alone and so you remain alone. Before you beat yourself up, know that dwelling on what we don't want couldn't be more natural. It is just simply a response that we, as humans, have to learn to engineer around. If you plant a garden of daisies, would you only water the weeds and expect the flowers to bloom? It's time for you to reverse this process, take control of your thoughts, and start focusing on what you want rather than what you don't want. Developing this habit will provide tremendous support for when you are ready to clarify your goals.

*The universe will always give you
what you ask for.*

Let's compare this methodology to destructive vibrations and constructive vibrations. Your thoughts are something very real. Just as your body is made up of tiny pulsating atoms and energy, thoughts are things composed of energetic matter. Your thoughts are vibrations on a non-physical level. These vibrations can manifest as happiness or fear, poverty or prosperity, health or disease. The path you set out to discover will reveal itself to be exactly what you expect and exactly what you are searching for. The universe deals in energy.

The vibration of your thoughts focuses on either having something or not having something, which tells the universe what to serve you. It is through these vibrations that you place the order in the first place. If you accept that your thoughts have the power to control your destiny, then you're in a unique position to achieve whatever dreams you set your mind to achieving. Through your focus, determination, and faith, the world truly is at your feet. Lisa and her team did not break the world sales record by allowing their thoughts to linger on how difficult it would be. They broke the record by focusing on how it could be done and taking the steps, faithfully, to do it.

Concrete goals provide us with opportunities to leave our comfort zone and really push ourselves to do something we have never done before. If you have a goal, and have faith in your goal, you'll most certainly be moved to action. Lisa and her team focused singularly on breaking the sales record...and did it.

By creating a specific goal and cementing it into reality through your thoughts, you are creating something real. You are creating something with your thoughts that did not exist prior to your thinking it into existence. By solidifying your goal, you are taking hold of the direction in which your life is moving by creating your next steps. When you do this, the result is always growth. As you create these goals, supercharged with the sheer magnitude of your faith, the steps to achieve them begin to present themselves in a very clear and concise way.

After a goal is established, the key is to apply unwavering faith. Know that the universe will give you what you seek. Believe in this truth every single day. Let your burning desire run free—not only on the first day when you begin, but every day that follows. You cannot simply apply faith on day one and then wonder where it will take you on day two.

Every day requires you to consciously apply faith to the goals on which you choose to focus your energies. Every single day has to be full of that burning desire to make your dreams a reality. Perseverance is necessary to your success and one of the essential secrets to realizing your goals. A "perseverance plan" for how to stay focused and faithful absolutely has to be a part of setting goals because your excitement will certainly dwindle at some point before you realize your goal.

You just have to start. What is it that you want to do? What are your dreams? Start there. Think your goal into existence. If the process seems too complex to begin, then you're overcomplicating it. To start is simple. If you have the goal that is tied to your purpose, then define it, believe in it, and it will move you to action.

Have you ever thought about why thinking this way is called a "leap of faith"? There is no empirical evidence of what is waiting for you on the other side. No Magic 8-Ball or looking glass shows you where the path may lead. Imagine standing on one side of a river bank. The trees and overgrown brush don't allow you to see what is on the other side of the river, but it is your dream to make it across the river and stand on the river bank on the opposite side. You are aware that the water will be choppy in places and that the undercurrent may be dangerous at times, but you are willing to take the risks to reach the other side because you believe you can. So you take a leap of faith, meaning you put every last bit of your faith into your own abilities.

Until you feel inspired to make that leap, every single day you must imagine yourself on the other side of that river. Focus on knowing that you can achieve this goal. Build up your strength to allow yourself to survive the treacherous water. You have identified the goal to cross the river, and now the steps to make it happen are becoming clearer by the day. The more you focus on your goal, the more you can see the steps you need to take to achieve it. The more you can have faith that you will accomplish your goal, the more likely you are to realize it. Period.

It seems simple, but this is how dreams become reality. **You start.** You take control of your thoughts. The dream to reach the other side of the river did not exist until you thought it into reality. You apply faith to those thoughts; then you take action. That first leap may be terrifying in the beginning, as it is totally based on faith, and you may not get to the other side on the first try. But you know you will get there eventually because you have faith in your abilities. So apply yourself, focus on the goal at hand, and do everything in your power to achieve your goal.

With each step you take, you gain clarity for the next step you will take. Once you reach the other side of the river bank, you will realize the adventure that the journey has brought you.

You will feel what it means to have accomplished something you brought to life with your own mind. You will realize the power your thoughts have on the world around you, when you simply apply them with dedicated focus and are brave enough to ask the universe for what you really want from life.

There is so much happening around you that is out of your control, and it is constant. However, your thoughts are never on that list, yet they may have the largest effect on your daily life. At times, it may be easier to choose not to control thoughts so you don't feel obligated or responsible to yourself. As we mentioned earlier, it's easier to be passive than it is to tune in. Rather than taking the path less traveled, we are wired to take *no path at all*, but this is not the path to gold and it never will be.

If you want to achieve a goal, you have to first believe that you can do it. You cannot be passive about where you may end up. You have to play an active role in deciding where you **will** end up. Every single day you let pass without taking that first step is equivalent to your agreeing that your dreams are not worth your effort. There is no limit to what you can do, and there is no one out there who can actually stop you. The responsibility to take an active path toward a purpose is resting solely on your shoulders. You must decide what you will do with your life. When you are passive in life, you are giving up your dreams. Period.

This is what fear wants from you. Fear wants to take away your dreams and your passions. Fear wants to take over your thoughts. Fear wants you to be passive and never choose a path because risk of failure is scary. Except, failure doesn't actually exist unless you allow it to exist. From every single experience you will learn and grow, whether or not the outcome is the one you expected. Your answer to fear is fully believing in your own capabilities, regardless of your past experiences or current expectations. Your leap of faith has to be so strong that no matter what fear has to say, your answer is *always*, "I can achieve this. I have faith in my abilities."

You can never give power to thoughts of giving up or failure.

You must put all negative thoughts out of your mind. Replace thoughts of "no," "not enough," and "never" with thoughts of "yes," "success," and "victory." Each day, imagine yourself living your dreams. Focus on the steps it will take to destroy negative thoughts until your path becomes inherently clear.

Just as we learned from John Assaraf, fear can be replaced with a positive emotion through pattern interruption. If you are able to set fear aside and replace it with something positive that serves your dreams rather than your stagnation, you will begin building the habit of staring at your dreams and becoming clear about what it is that you truly want to achieve. From this point on, you can accomplish anything.

Your story, your life, and your achievements are waiting as thoughts, ready to become your new reality. Will you choose to give those thoughts life? Are you ready and courageous enough to apply faith to your goals to allow them to become your reality?

If your answer is a resounding "Yes!" here's how you start today:

1. **Define your true purpose:** Before you can start setting goals, you need to know where you want to end up...and what you want to accomplish along the way.

2. **Choose your goal:** What do you want to achieve? Identify exactly what you want. Write your goal on a piece of paper and keep it with you at all times. Read your goal every morning and every night to ensure your focus stays in the right place. As you move closer toward your vision, you can update this to reflect exactly where you are in life.

3. **Set your strategy:** You absolutely must set specific and clear deadlines. How can you use what you've learned thus far to achieve this goal? How can you allow your thoughts to work for you, rather than against you? Outline each step you believe you need to take, and update your strategy, as needed, as you grow with your goal.

4. **Take action:** What is one thing you can do today, based on your strategy, that will put you closer to achieving your goal? Rome wasn't built in a day. You won't build your dream life in a day either. You don't have to do it all at once; just begin. If you set aside one hour per day, or even just 20 minutes, over the course of a year you will have spent a considerable amount of time on your dreams.

5. **Apply faith:** Constantly. On good days and on bad days. You have to believe and know you can accomplish the goals you've laid out, or you never will. It's that simple. As time

passes, you must continue applying faith. You must continue to believe in yourself and where you are going in life.

6. **Repeat:** Tomorrow is a new day. Every day will require you to focus on creating thoughts that are supportive of what you want to achieve. You have to keep that burning desire alive. You have to want to succeed just as much on day thirty as you do on day one. Repetition is key.

If you pour faith into your purpose, your goals, and yourself, you can achieve your dreams. You have to believe and know you can do it even before you know how you can do it.

The only limitations that exist are the ones we put on ourselves. The universe is not limiting you or your dreams. It is simply waiting for you to take action.

*Are you ready to allow yourself to start
and keep "crushing it"?*

Chapter Three

Overcoming Obstacles

*Learning to learn is very close to
learning how to earn.*

What may hold us back from truly "crushing it"? We all have one area in our lives where we don't conform, or where we struggle—for some it is with public speaking, others with numbers and accounting. For some, the struggles are inherited at birth through a life of poverty or a lack of opportunities or education. These hurdles can be difficult to overcome, and the past can carry baggage and beliefs that, try as we might, drag us down in all our endeavors.

We are in an era of extremes. Some families enjoy wealth and abundance and have access to experiences, while some families struggle just to feed and house their children. Obviously, this would put families in poverty at a disadvantage, making a bad situation seemingly impossible to overcome and thereby creating obstacles that are passed from one generation to the next.

Being privileged isn't anything new, but neither is being at a disadvantage. Napoleon Hill studied both while conducting research for *Think and Grow Rich.* Hill uncovered several subjects who had overcome major obstacles and ultimately created success. He left us with this reminder: "Remember, too, that all who succeed in life get off to a bad start and pass through many heartbreaking struggles before they arrive. The turning point in the lives of those who succeed usually comes at some moment of crisis, through which they are introduced to their 'other selves.'"

We've all heard of successful individuals who overcame great struggles in their quest to success. Motivational speaker and bestselling author Les Brown grew up in poverty. In addition, he was a hyperactive child who was placed in special education classes throughout grade school and high school. Yet despite multiple disadvantages, he managed to turn what others would call a difficult childhood into a life where he has enjoyed highly successful careers in broadcasting, public speaking, television, and politics.

For every person who is slated to be the most likely to succeed, there is another at the opposite end of the spectrum who can be labeled least likely to succeed. Among the latter, we found some very inspirational and successful entrepreneurs who overcame the odds and proved that success isn't a byproduct of their childhood status or their past weaknesses.

Meet Brian Sidorsky. Brian is a Canadian who came from a poor, humble, and, by his definition, dysfunctional family. He describes himself as a once-fragile child who was most likely diabetic during much of his childhood, though he wasn't diagnosed until much later. He also states that he was a poor student—a very, very poor student.

Things began to turn around when he was a teenager. At the age of 15, he discovered Junior Achievement, which he credits with making him very keen on learning how to do business. Brian shares his story:

"Although I was a terrible student, I studied *Think and Grow Rich* and read it hundreds of times. Through learning and applying the principles in that book, I was not only successful in my Junior Achievement company, but I started my own secondhand furniture and appliance business when I was 20 years old. A year later, I was selling both new and used furniture and appliances when I was 21 years old. By the time I was 23, I opened what would soon be the largest retail furniture and appliance store in Calgary, doing over a million dollars a month in volume and employing over 25 salespeople.

"That success was due to the training I had in Junior Achievement—it certainly had nothing to do with what I'd learned in school. Junior Achievement teaches experiential learning— learning by doing—which was how I learned to learn in a way that I could comprehend."

Brian attributes his success to applying the principle of having a definite purpose. By the time he reached the age of 30, he had made his first million dollars. When he was 35, he sold his store to the largest retailer in Canada—it was 1981 and interest rates were 22 percent. Essentially, Brian could make a million dollars a year by staying home.

But he didn't. He went back to school, but first he hired a high school teacher to help him with the subjects that had been difficult for him. He knew he wasn't ready for a college education—conventional classroom studies had never been his forte.

With instruction, he figured out how to overcome his learning obstacles and become a commendable student. He then went on to attend the University of Calgary, and while he was there he realized that everyone was there to get a degree so they could get a job—but he didn't want to get a job; he wanted to be the person who gave jobs to others.

After just one year, Brian began developing mobile home parks and shopping centers. Through land development, he turned five million dollars of net worth into 700 million dollars in assets.

A terrible student by his own admission, Brian soaks up every piece of education and knowledge he can find. Today, he reads three to five books every week—quite a feat for someone who didn't like school. "I love reading about anything, particularly philosophy and psychology. However, I read electrical and mechanical manuals, architecture, engineering, design, and even books about art and painting. I want to learn everything there is to know about everything. I want to be a know-it-all. I'm constantly looking for new information—the new key to success."

Brian is on a journey to learn the new key to success, but we wanted to know what the key was to his own success. How did a struggling student become not only an avid learner, but a wildly successful entrepreneur? Brian's answer was not only unique; it was also very insightful.

"Be willing to learn *how* to learn. Learning how to learn is very close to learning how to earn. The more I learn, the more I know that I don't know. The more I know that I don't know, the more I want to learn. Not only do I want to learn, but I want to apply it and see it actualized. I want to go from reading and becoming that person who can do those things I have learned to being someone who can pass those results on to other people."

Be willing to learn how to learn—that wisdom has transformed Brian Sidorsky from a poor student to a profound teacher. By taking action, he overcame a childhood of poverty and stopped the cycle that ensnares many bright young minds. Brian turned education from being his biggest weakness to being his greatest strength.

Napoleon Hill understood the importance of learning when he said, "The way of success is the way of continuous pursuit of knowledge." **That knowledge doesn't necessarily require years of postsecondary formal studies in the pursuit of a degree that can be framed and hung on the wall. Knowledge can come to us in many forms, including hands-on training, videos, books, and mentors.** Through *Think and Grow Rich*, Napoleon Hill served as one of Brian's teachers, and it has made a tremendous impact on Brian's attitude and success. Brian even states that he makes one million dollars every time he reads it.

The world is abundant with knowledge that is accessible at our fingertips...if we choose to seek and use it. As in everything, the choices we make determine our results. Regardless of our limitations, backgrounds, or unforeseen obstacles that present themselves, we can still be in control of the outcome because we have the power to choose differently.

Brian could have done like so many would have and chosen to give up on school and on learning. After all, he knew he wasn't a stellar student and didn't enjoy school. He chose instead to turn this deficit into a strength. Once he realized he had the power to change his circumstances and results, he opened doors that had once been impenetrable.

"The power that came to me would be the power to choose. When I was very despondent and suffering from self-victimization and stinking thinking, I heard Dr. Wayne Dyer say, 'When you can control your thoughts, you can control your feelings.' If you can control your feelings, you can control your life. The power to choose everything in life is the one thing people don't understand; therefore, they think that circumstances and life affect them. But it's how they choose to respond to those that's important."

What is the right response? Brian says it should always be positive. In his early days, he would think something was wrong when life was good. In turn, he'd do something to sabotage it. Today, he realizes that his life can be positive, positive, positive—that doesn't have to pause.

Always on the lookout for what could go wrong, people overlook what could go right. When something good happens, they let negative possibilities creep into their thoughts and wait for the proverbial other shoe to drop. Negativity breeds inactivity. As Napoleon Hill said, "A positive mind finds a way it can be done; a negative mind looks for all the ways it can't be done."

Through the power of choice, we get to determine the results we want and the means to achieve those results. The average individual makes as many as a dozen choices before they go to the work in the morning. Often, though, we overlook the choices that are available, thereby significantly limiting ourselves and the options we have. Choice is more than the ability to choose—it's about consciously researching and exploring options in order to make the best choice for our particular needs. That's where the "power" of choice comes in—by exercising our ability to choose, we have the ability to steer results in the direction intended. It puts us in power, rather than letting the situation or circumstance have power over us.

Through his knowledge and the power of choice, Brian has done much more than create success—he's metabolized success. He doesn't just read a book; he absorbs it, underlines it, chews it up, and rereads it again and again. Metabolize is a 25-dollar word, but when you metabolize something, you bring it into your cellular system. When you metabolize information, it becomes a part of you and everything you do.

Learning how to learn and metabolizing what he's learned has enriched Brian with many life experiences, starting with Junior Achievement. Through Junior Achievement, the door to learning opened for Brian, who is now the founder and CEO of Lansdowne Equity Ventures Ltd., a highly profitable real estate business with operations in land banking, real estate development, and property management of commercial shopping centers and mobile home parks. Through Junior Achievement, Brian learned a valuable lesson—that anyone can overcome adversity and have what they want in life. Be strong in your belief that you can achieve your wildest dreams. There will be obstacles and adversity; that is normal. You will learn more from your failures than your successes, but those will be the stepping stones toward future seeds and benefits of success in your life.

Brian has experienced failures. His furniture business had grown at such a rapid clip that he was undercapitalized and unable to pay his suppliers on time. He addressed the issue, explaining that he was having trouble paying on time, and he created a payment schedule with his suppliers. Instead of letting circumstances have the power to control his results, he adopted a positive perspective, reviewed his choices, and took control of the situation. Brian knows that opportunity is often disguised as temporary defeat or misfortune. With each setback, he has exercised his power to use the incident as an opportunity to gain and metabolize knowledge and take back his power to control his results.

We've all heard the line, or what is sometimes used as an excuse, "I didn't have a choice." We always have choices, and the biggest choice we will ever make is choosing to consciously exercise the power of choice. Brian chose to master learning, which has been the most difficult thing for him. He credits Junior Achievement with teaching him how to learn, and today he serves on the board of Junior Achievement. It was the stepping stone that whet his insatiable appetite for learning. Learning is an everyday choice for Brian. It's the magic key to his success. It was always available to him, but it wasn't accessible until he learned how to learn that he was able to unlock the vault of knowledge that turned his life around.

A book is not the best teacher. The best teacher is the one who teaches the student how to read a book.

We know that if you give a man a fish, he will eat for a day, but if you teach a man to fish, he will eat every day. Similarly, if you teach someone how to learn, they will learn for a lifetime. The willingness and ability to continually learn makes any obstacle surmountable.

Failure is imminent—it's what you do after you fail that counts.

There is this idea that when things don't go exactly as we expect them to, we have failed. It is also too common that when we are met with setbacks or failures, we believe that we are not meant to continue and so we throw in the towel. Failure is inevitable. It is an integral part of the learning and growth process, and without failure your success wouldn't quite look the same. If Brian had not experienced failure and difficulty in school, he would not be the person he is today.

In fact, we can take that one step further by saying failure is vital in the process of finding success. If you learn to switch your mind-set to use setbacks to propel you forward rather than allowing setbacks to stop you in your tracks, you will change the way you live. When giving up is not an option, your perception of the setback and the job of that setback changes immediately. Rather than a failure being an end to the path you are on, it becomes a fork in the road, revealing new paths to you, allowing you to change direction in that moment.

Your life isn't about the day you fail.
It's about the day after.

Napoleon Hill once said, "Before success comes in any man's life, he is sure to meet with temporary defeat, and, perhaps, some failure.... Failure is a trickster with a keen sense of irony and cunning. It takes great delight in tripping one when success is almost within reach."

The most successful men in this world will tell you that their successes have always come in the steps after their failures. If they had let their defeat win, and take over their lives, they would have never realized their dreams. Brian's growth in his furniture company came on the edge of catastrophic consequences from the undercapitalization in his business.

Failure is imminent. You absolutely will fail or experience setbacks. But your life is not about the day you fail. It is about the day after you fail—and the days, weeks, and months after that. It is what you do with your failures and your setbacks that will determine the course of your life.

When you see a climber at the peak of a mountain, you know only of their success. You see them in celebration, cheerful about their well-earned victory. You did not see their struggles to make it to the summit. That climber could easily tell you exactly how many times their foot slipped or recount what injuries and hardships they suffered throughout their journey up the mountain.

It is silly and naive to assume that others have an easier path, free and clear of setbacks, on their journey to success.

Our brains use this trick to rationalize throwing in the proverbial towel by working to convince us that we are not able to accomplish the challenge at hand. When fear of failure takes hold of your thought process, it tells you that you are not good enough and *that* is why *you* have failed while others have succeeded. The truth is that everyone suffers failures and setbacks. Everyone experiences struggles. Your ultimate success is determined by how you choose to deal with failure.

Nobody is immune to failure.

When you always look forward in a very positive manner, it's hard to be discouraged about where you've been or where you are going. As you continue moving forward, your progress will allow you to identify the importance of each success and failure and their role in landing you exactly where you are right now.

When giving up is not an option, your perception and the job of failure changes.

Our human instincts cause almost everyone to shy away from anything that produces negative feelings or emotions. What if you decided to shine a light on these perceived failures in your life? What if you illuminate your setbacks to gain absolute clarity?

You would be free to learn everything you possibly could from each setback or failure and to truly use those moments to propel your life forward.

Most people suffering a major loss would hide under a rock. We aren't taught to shine a light on our problems for the world to easily see. It is so easy to take the "woe is me" path, to claim victim status, rather than to take a good look at what went wrong, accept it, learn from it, and move forward.

There is a remarkable amount of science behind this as well. Your brain is not linear and organized in its processes. It is, essentially, a prediction engine that is designed to learn through trial and error. Our brains have evolved to predict, fail, and then repeat until something sticks. When you consider failures in this way, it becomes clear how valuable your setbacks are because they are wiring your brain for future success. Simply put, with each setback comes wisdom and knowledge you will be able to apply later in life to avoid similar situations.

There are a million rags-to-riches stories out there, and this process of learning from failure is why. If you continue throwing a noodle at a wall, eventually it will stick somewhere. When you fear failure, you deny yourself the opportunity to grow through trial and error. Like Brian did, if you learn to accept that failure is part of the learning process, you will achieve success.

The act of trying and failing is incredibly valuable to your eventual success.

As you try and fail, you gain a greater conceptual understanding of exactly what you are doing. Once you develop this deeper understanding of the real opportunity for learning in each failure or setback, this pattern of learning will be cemented in your brain and will apply itself to all areas of your life. This is unique because when you are told or taught something, the knowledge is embedded differently and even stored in a different part of your brain than if you were to learn that same information through trial and error. In the simplest terms possible: you are getting smarter with each failure or setback.

Acknowledging your setbacks allows your brain to learn the lesson in the setback and then move on. As soon as this happens, the sting of failure fades from your memory and it gets replaced with the lesson(s). Unacknowledged failures tend to sit and fester as they spread negativity to other areas of your life.

As Napoleon Hill so cleverly said, "Every adversity, every failure, and every heartache carries with it the seed of an equivalent or greater benefit." Every adversity...every failure...every heartache...all working in your life, to serve the purpose of moving you closer toward the jackpot—success and happiness most people only dream about.

Are you ready to allow your journey to become unforgettable? Are you ready to seek transparency and meet your setbacks head-on?

What's a recent setback you've experienced? How can you use that setback to move yourself closer to your dreams? Here's your magic key to success in the face of failure:

1. **Be honest:** One of the hardest things in life is being honest with ourselves. The more willing you are to take a close look at where you are, how you got there, and where you plan to go, the better you play your hand in the next round.

2. **Illuminate:** Transparency will serve you well in life, especially when applied to your setbacks. Instead of hiding from failure, shine a bright light on what you are doing—so much so that you can see and understand every aspect of what happened. There is no teacher like life. Extracting the valuable lessons from each setback will only contribute to your success.

3. **Discuss:** It's okay to talk about what went wrong. Shying away from negativity is a natural reaction for all of us, so you must work to change that in yourself. Rather than avoiding your negative experience, talk about it and figure out how to make it a positive by learning from it.

4. **Take action:** Now that you've identified where you went wrong, use that knowledge and awareness to take the next step forward. You should always be in action, taking steps toward your next big play. If failure knocks you down, you don't have to stay there.

5. **Repeat:** Aspire to get so good at failing that you learn to do it without ever actually stopping. Using each experience helps you stay eight or nine steps ahead. If you aren't failing at all, you aren't taking enough risks and you aren't training your brain.

When you learn how to use the setback as the reason to accomplish something, you will experience a shift. Whether we feel shame, anger, embarrassment, defeat, or devastation, no one likes to hit a roadblock. That's why you have to keep moving forward, turning that roadblock into an opportunity to take the next fork in the road and change your direction.

Failure feels bad because you aren't designed to fail. You aren't designed to accept shame or anger or even defeat. You are designed to succeed and enjoy the jackpot. We must fail in order to succeed. We have to fail to realize how badly we want something, to keep pushing for it. We have to fail to take a step back to reevaluate where we are just before we get what we've been playing for. We have to fail to gain the wisdom necessary to live a life of abundance; to play our best hand yet.

Failure is inevitable. It is an integral part of the learning and growth process, and without failure your success wouldn't quite look the same.

Chapter Four

Find the Gap

Necessity is the mother of all invention.

As our society evolves, we are driven more and more to create. In the business world, it is critical to seek out gaps in the marketplace and then strive to create solutions to fill these unaddressed needs. Problem solvers by nature, entrepreneurs feel a deep yearning to offer new solutions and ideas to an ever-changing economy.

As our society and economy continually change, one fact does not: necessity is the mother of all invention. Where an unaddressed need exists, a gap waits to be filled by the curiosity and creativity of someone willing to take on the task. John Ashworth is exactly the kind of person who can recognize an unaddressed gap and simultaneously visualize the best way to fill it. His talent first revealed itself at a young age. He loved golf but hated the attire. The emotion of hating golf attire was eventually enough to drive him into action.

Early on, John played golf as a hobby. He later traveled the country working as a caddy on the tour. He loved everything about his job, with the exception of the awful clothing required to play the sport. John never considered how his attention to the clothing would later shape his life and serve as the foundation to his success. John didn't realize it at the time, but he had uncovered a huge existing gap in the golf clothing marketplace. His distaste for the standard clothing shifted to imagining solutions, his entrepreneurial spirit already shaping his thought process.

After a few odd jobs, John found himself working as a buyer and was able to see all of the clothing lines available for sale at the time. Again, his entrepreneurial thought process was kicking in. His love–hate relationship with the sports attire available in the market picked back up and began replanting the seed in his mind that perhaps he was the right person to tackle this problem. He was recognizing a gap in the marketplace.

When the company for which John was working as a buyer was about to go out of business, John started taking a closer look at what his next steps would be and where he wanted to go in life. He was still young, but his desire to choose a path about which he was passionate was really pulling at him. It made sense to John to focus a career around golf, the game he loved, but without being a paid golfer, what did that look like?

For John, before he was John Ashworth of Ashworth Clothing, that next step looked like bringing something new to the market. John developed an innovative line of golf attire unlike anything previously available on the market. And consumers went crazy. They hadn't realized they were longing for this improved sportswear until John so wisely delivered it. For John, he felt that the existing clothing was a poor representation of a truly wonderful game. He even thought that the clothing really distracted from the prestige of the game. To John, everything looked the same, and he craved something new that would mirror the sophistication and elegance of the sport, along with the people who play it. He set out to create something that he would be proud to wear and put his name on.

There is a specific reason why some products make a page in the history books of consumerism and others never see the light of day. Viral products are born from an existing place of necessity. Entrepreneurs who learn how to create within the gap of necessity find success. The best products are the result of someone looking at what the market has to offer to a specific target audience and having the vision to see the difference between what the market is offering versus what people actually want and, most importantly, need. These are the products that consumers want, and they take off because they are useful and desired. Having the ability to give someone something they didn't know they wanted or needed until you put it in front of them is a magical thing.

The golf industry has been around for 500 years, and it has experienced transition every step of the way. Markets evolve as our needs, desires, and understanding advance. Every market undergoes change as gaps grow between what exists and what consumers grow to want and need over time. Inventions and designs allow us to expand our horizons, evolve faster than ever before, and, in John's case, look good while doing it.

Right now, a lot of creation focuses on reducing human effort to simplify life or to make life more enjoyable. Inventions must fall into one of these categories to find success.

Where there's a will, there's a way.

Difficult situations, or situations lacking resources, always seem to inspire ingenious solutions. When the need for something becomes essential, it pushes you in the direction of getting or achieving the desired solution. When we see the focus shift to a real, actual need, something that is missing on the market, this is when we really see innovation at its best. Finding this gap is when entrepreneurs start to push forward in all directions.

The very first golf ball was made of thin leather and stuffed with feathers. A modern golf ball is designed with incredibly careful detail. Even the number of dimples is specific to allow the ball to travel further while reducing turbulence. Innovation is in everything we touch, from the shirt we put on to go golfing all the way down to the ball we hit and the tee we use to prop that ball up. The golf ball perfectly illustrates innovation in the marketplace because the desire of golfers to lower their handicap left a gap for more aerodynamic balls. A new space for innovative design came about, and now an entire industry exists based on this singular gap.

As we are innovating faster than ever before in response to rapidly evolving markets, we are constantly learning that this is a formula for inventing in this needs-based gap. Understanding this formula will help to accelerate you forward. The formula relies on the creative process and will push the limits of your ability to think outside the box. This allows you to free your mind and tap into a new way of thinking and approaching needs in the market.

Entrepreneurs see their passion and their purpose as part of something they must do, a task they must complete, a mountain they must climb. So when we talk about necessity, this is necessity on more than one level. There is also a primary level of necessity from the entrepreneurs themselves to create and give to the world, or at least their world. Entrepreneurs feel compelled to offer of themselves to make a difference. This is a separate kind of necessity. This necessity fills a gap inside the entrepreneur and allows a separate purpose to be fulfilled.

When it comes to the life of an entrepreneur, curiosity is a major component, and it's also a significant part of the creative process when filling market gaps. Some of the most successful people you'll ever meet are incredibly curious about everything they touch and see. Intelligence and curiosity go hand in hand. The smartest people, who are constantly innovating and creating, are always learning something new. They are always asking questions and exploring the world around them. Curiosity, in so many ways, makes the world go 'round.

There's a story we love to retell about a man who really had the world at his feet. His office had an incredible skyline view, his car wasn't hurting for horsepower, and his house was the mansion of all mansions. You can imagine the surprise, as we were golfing together one day, when he went into the water after a ball. Not on the edge of the water, or even ankle deep— he actually walked deep into the water to retrieve a three-dollar ball. Heck, he probably owned half the stock in the golf company, along with hundreds of those balls. When he came out of the water, we were all gathered around and couldn't help but laugh a little because he was absolutely soaked from the waist down. Nobody could believe he had gone in after his ball and, of course, we had to ask him why. "What in the world are you doing?" someone asked between laughs. His reply was priceless: "I have been working hard on my swing. I wanted to know exactly how far my ball went." That was that, and he walked back to the golf cart without thinking any more about it.

Curiosity truly does make the world go 'round. You would never have the ability to understand the necessities or the gaps in any market if you weren't curious enough to find out. This is true for everything you touch. Think of a child and how they interact with the world around them. They want to touch everything, to feel everything, to grab and hold everything. Children do not shy away from anything, because they have not yet been patterned with knowledge of fear. Instead, they are just curious. They need to know what everything is, how it works, whether or not it comes apart, and even sometimes...what it tastes like.

Entrepreneurs—true entrepreneurs who are changing the world—have managed to hold onto a higher level of curiosity, and this serves their success daily. It doesn't have to apply only to business either. Curiosity touches every aspect of life, and the continuous hunger for knowledge and understanding allows you to acquire more from life—not necessarily in terms of material things, but rather in terms of mental aptitude. Your abilities, your talents, and your skills reach further and further as you learn and grow and as that knowledge encompasses more of the world.

This increased level of curiosity allows you to keep an active mind, rather than being a passive figure in your own life. Curiosity encourages you to ask questions, to seek out more answers, to recognize opportunities, to look below the surface and see more. When you are tuned in and you are taking an active interest in the world around you, you can begin to recognize opportunities and gaps in the markets around you. This point is when the pieces will begin to fall into place for you and when you will find yourself being elevated to new, higher levels of success as your understanding of the world around you solidifies.

Think about it...the most curious people out there are the true problem solvers. They are asking the right questions because they care. They have an actual vested interest in changing the world around them. Curious people desire this change and to be a vehicle of it. How about the curious people you know? Are you one of them? Do you take a vested interest in the world around you? Do you ask a lot of questions? Are you willing to get all the way in the water if that's what it takes to get your answers?

The formula we mentioned earlier starts with curiosity. You must be curious, interested, and ready to solve a problem in order to recognize the market gap you wish to fill.

If necessity is the mother of all invention, curiosity is the father.

This is the desire we've talked about in earlier chapters. This formula for success envelops the passion and the drive it takes to find success as an entrepreneur. John is a great example of what happens when someone applies the formula for success we are discussing. His curiosity was the foundation for what he calls "passion play" into the market of golf attire. John talks a lot about his creative and imaginative thought process and how he leaves everything on the table. He questions every last detail. There is no "I can't" or "That won't work." Rather, it's a more fun process of "What if we did?" or "Why not try?"

This kind of creative process, teamed with curiosity, has cemented John's place in the world of golf. He has changed the course of his legacy, and his family's legacy...what we're talking about here is huge. Creativity combined with curiosity should never be discounted or looked at as "not a big deal." This formula changed John's life, and as a result, he has changed the lives of thousands of people with whom he has come in contact. The ripple in the pond...you never know exactly how far an idea will take you. But if you aren't curious enough to find out, that idea won't take you anywhere.

Our conversations with John have yielded some wonderful insights on this formula for success. Identifying gaps in the market, along with the overall mind-set you apply to the discovery of those gaps, are incredibly important to success.

We travel the world and are grateful for the opportunity to talk to people from all walks of life. It always seems to come back to this simple idea: if you are curious, if you want it bad enough, if you are willing to stay the course, you will find success. This is the formula.

Let's go back to necessity and finding gaps in the market. This idea of necessity being the mother of all invention changes a bit when we bring curiosity into the mixture. Another trait that seems to go hand in hand with curiosity is open-mindedness, having the ability to consider all options on the table—and even some that aren't quite on the table or don't even exist yet. Inquisitive people are able to generate more ideas simply by being open-minded and asking questions that will move them closer to possible solutions or answers.

The best and the brightest, the elite, the top dogs...they know this formula, they practice it, and they have found success in their lives by applying their curiosity coupled with open-mindedness. You possess the same capabilities to learn and apply these behaviors to your daily life. They are thinking and existing on a higher level daily. Whether or not you will choose to do the same is completely up to you. You have opportunities every single day to take the swing, chase your ball, and maybe even decide to get in the water to go after what you want. Every swing won't be a hole-in-one, and there will be plenty of rough patches along the way. But the more you push forward, the more you learn the course, the more curious you become, the more likely you are to find lasting success and happiness. This is how champions are created. We already know there is a champion inside of you.

Are you ready to tee up?

Chapter Five

The Power of Asking

***Ask people what they need
and give them that.***

We've spent a lot of time talking to business coaches around the world, and one of the most interesting things we've discovered in these conversations is the importance of asking questions. In fact, this is a repetitive theme throughout the entire coaching industry. The foundation for every good coach is an arsenal of powerful questions, which, when asked at just the right moment, are designed to generate "aha" moments and major breakthroughs. What we've learned is that this philosophy of asking questions can easily be applied to business for tremendous success.

Knowing this, we were not surprised to hear that the success formula for Michael Houlihan and Bonnie Harvey was a system based on questions. With both of their backgrounds in business coaching, they knew the importance of asking questions, and it helped them to build the No. 1 selling wine brand in the world. Now, you must be wondering, *What kind of question is so great that it can build the No. 1 selling wine brand in the world?* We'll get to that in a minute, and it will blow your mind.

Perhaps you've heard of a little company called Barefoot Wine? Before Barefoot Wine became the huge, well-known brand it is, with the easily recognizable foot on the label, the brand actually lived in Michael and Bonnie's laundry room. Building what Michael refers to as their "get-rich-slow scheme," the two entrepreneurs set out to gain footing in the wine industry without an ounce of knowledge about wine other than the usual glass they enjoyed with dinner.

Both Michael and Bonnie are firm believers in being resourceful. Sometimes this was by choice, and other times it was for survival, especially in the cutthroat world of business and entrepreneurship. Rather than amassing buildings and other material items—a fancy warehouse, offices, storefronts, etc.—they believed in simplicity. They decided early on that their love of business could travel through any vehicle. In this case, the vehicle was wine, and that was really all they needed to start out. Well, that, and a modest space to run daily business operations. They both agreed the laundry room would do just fine, and they got to work.

Rather than jumping into the wine industry as wine experts, Michael and Bonnie took a totally different approach than anything we've ever seen. They armed themselves with every question you could ask any person in the industry, and they got to asking. This really is the opposite of how most entrepreneurs jump into business. A lot of people build brands they are in love with and then send them off into the world to live or die. Michael and Bonnie decided to change it up and go directly to their customers and just ask them what they wanted. With that information, they built a brand with which they knew their customers would fall in love.

When Barefoot Wine hit the market, there was no question of whether it would live or die, because they gave their customers exactly what they said they wanted. Talk about simplicity. It seems like there are a million websites and businesses out there dedicated to helping you find out what your customer might want from you...but what is stopping you from going directly to the source? How do you get to know the other guy? How do you come to understand what your customers want from you? By asking great questions.

We can even take that one step further by using the answers from these questions to put ourselves in their shoes. By becoming the customer and using the direct information, you really have to understand what they want from you. So, let's go back to our earlier question: What kind of question is so great that it can build the No. 1 selling wine brand in the world? The question that puts you in your customer's shoes.

This is really the opposite of human nature because typically we are tellers. We want to share what we know. Our entire lives, we are taught that being the teller, not the asker, gives us power over the situation. Our bosses, our teachers, even our parents, throughout our lives, never wanted questions but always demanded answers. So very early on, we developed this habit of needing to have answers and, even more than that, needing to share them.

As you can see from the rags-to-riches story of Barefoot Wine, being the asker also holds tremendous power. This approach allowed Michael and Bonnie to eliminate so much of the gray area that existed in an industry they really knew nothing about simply by putting themselves in the shoes of their customers. By being the askers, they were able to recognize a gap in a multibillion-dollar industry and then immediately fill it with a brand their consumers would purchase over and over.

Rather than going to their potential customers and telling them what they had, Michael and Bonnie went to those potential customers and asked them what they wanted. Their focus was to talk about the value they could provide for their customers. Not the product, or flavor, or even the quality of their wine—just what was in it for the customer, what need they had that a potential new wine brand could fill, and exactly how Michael and Bonnie could provide all of that in a way that made sense. Every last detail of Barefoot Wine is based on information that came directly from potential customers and people in the industry through a diligent process of asking (a lot of) questions and applying that information directly to their brand.

> *Forget about your product—let's take a*
> *closer look at your consumer.*

By learning, very early on, how to put themselves in everyone else's shoes, Bonnie and Michael perfected their sales formula. As Michael so wisely put it, "There are a lot of different pairs of shoes, and you've got to put yourself in every last pair because if not, you'll miss something that is so important to the process.

I wouldn't say that we are problem solvers. We just asked what people needed and figured we would give them that."

With a label that pays homage to the original winemaking process, flavors designed for consistent wine drinkers, and accessibility in every major store out there, it seems the process of asking has paid off in ways Michael and Bonnie were only dreaming of 20 years ago.

Their backgrounds in the business coaching world served them well because they understood the importance of questions designed to lead to discovery. After asking everyone in the wine industry—from the forklift drivers to the line managers—what they thought they needed to be successful, Michael and Bonnie were equipped with incredible information to build their brand.

When they made it through that part of the process and they had the brand ready to deliver, they focused their questions in other directions. For each challenge they faced they asked questions for clarity and used that information to turn those challenges into another aspect of their success story. They spent 20 years growing Barefoot Wine into the global brand it is today before selling it to the Gallo wine family. Twenty years adds up to *a lot* of questions, but seeing how the story turned out, it would be hard to believe that every last question wasn't worth the time spent asking.

Michael and Bonnie discovered something very valuable through their exploration in the business world: there is always more to learn. Asking great questions is the easiest way—the path of least resistance—to gain the knowledge you seek to help propel your business in the right direction. Most people, in most industries, are ready and willing to share their knowledge, because as we shared earlier, we are tellers, which means all you have to do is ask.

This goes hand in hand with everything we talked about in chapter 4. Curiosity to ask questions led this team of business coaches on a journey they could have never fathomed, yet selling Barefoot Wine to the Gallo wine family was not the end of their journey. It is not lost on Michael and Bonnie the tremendous lessons they learned along the way, and they have made it their passion to share those lessons with whomever wants to receive them.

Business was always their passion. The vehicle may have changed, but the duo is still traveling the world speaking of their love of business and truly enjoying every minute of it. They are sharing their success story globally with hopeful entrepreneurs and business lovers alike, with the goal of inspiring people to take action in their lives.

So, if great questions are the biggest part of Michael and Bonnie's magic key, how can you emulate that for maximum results? There's an art to asking effective questions, and you must get it right if you intend to get in the other person's shoes. In order for you to successfully emulate and apply this, you need to be able to ask specific, targeted questions that will draw out the answers you are seeking.

The danger in not being able to ask great questions is this: when we don't ask, we assume, and when we assume...it's easy to get it wrong. We've watched so many businesses and entrepreneurs fall flat just because they made assumptions about who their client was and what that customer wanted rather than putting in the time to find out the truth.

Another very important aspect of asking questions is the effect this process has as you learn every possible detail. All of the people who were answering Michael's and Bonnie's questions about their potential wine brand were actually mentally taking ownership with each answer they provided. Their answers were allowing them to invest intellectually in the potential company before it had even been born yet. As the product became real, every single one of those people felt responsible, in some way, for the success of the brand. Even if it was on a minor scale and even when the company didn't belong to them, that urge to make it work existed inside of each one of them.

When we have invested in something, whether it is financially or intellectually, we have created a connection, and that is the true genius of this approach. With each question asked, Michael and Bonnie were essentially creating the largest team any brand has ever seen and simultaneously generating a massive amount of energy around their soon-to-be brand.

As soon as you are able to completely master the art of asking questions, you will begin experiencing more beneficial, longer-lasting connections and relationships that will, in turn, allow you to create more value for your clients, for yourself, and for your business. The questions we ask will determine the overall quality of our relationships but also our problem-solving abilities, our curiosity, and our creativity—all of which are key components of our overall success.

ASKING POWERFUL QUESTIONS.

1. **Choose wisely:** Open-ended questions (Why do you like this?) are always a better option than closed-ended (Do you like this?) questions. Closed-ended questions usually result in a "yes" or "no" response while open-ended questions allow the conversation to go in almost any direction. So, try to focus on "what" or "how" questions. A great question should be effective and thought provoking. Here are a few examples of great questions:

    a. What do you make of __________?

    b. How do you feel about __________?

    c. What can you tell me regarding __________?

    d. How would you handle __________?

2. **Practice patience:** A huge part of effective communication is actually learning to be quiet. It's normal to want to fill the silence, but it's important to learn to practice patience and wait for the answers you are seeking. The less you say, the more you hear. Allow the answers to come at their own speed.

3. **Allow the answer to develop:** A lot of times the answer for which you are looking doesn't actually exist yet. It will develop and grow as the conversation grows. Don't make the common mistake of ending or interrupting the answering process too soon. Allow time for the conversation to grow organically as the exchange goes on. You should be in no hurry.

4. **Remain curious:** Again, with the curiosity...we know, we know. But it truly is an integral part of the questioning process. The point is this: never assume you know what anyone's answer will be. If you go into a conversation with this mind-set, you are sure to miss a lot of what's being said. Use your curiosity to hear, and then follow-up with even deeper discovery questions.

5. **Forget the power play:** Listen, we know you're intelligent; you know you're intelligent. During a discovery conversation is the worst time to try and put your smarts on display. You must be willing to forgo control of the conversation to effectively question and gather information. Forget the power play and focus instead on listening. When you are really listening, you will tune into different levels of emotional, verbal, and nonverbal communication.

THE NEXT STEPS

So, let's say you've mastered the art of asking, you're in front of a potential client, and you ask your first question. What happens next is so imperative to the success of the process, and that is: how good you are at receiving their answer. We are never really taught to be good listeners. We are told to listen a lot but not coached on how to actually do that, so most of us fumble through life missing a lot of what is being said, simply because we don't know how to tune in. We've all heard the saying, "If you're not listening, you're not learning," and it couldn't be truer when applied to business. You may be equipped with the best questions in the world, but if you aren't capable of receiving the answers to those questions, what's the point?

In earlier chapters, we talked about mastering your thoughts, and this is a time when that skill will prove to be incredibly important. A lot of the time we are in a constant cycle of talking and then, rather than listening, thinking of what we will say or contribute next. In order to break this cycle, you must become the master of your mind and learn to quiet those thoughts so that after every question you ask, you are truly ready to receive the answer.

> ***To be a good listener takes practice. To be a great listener takes patience.***

Your full attention will allow you to hear everything that is being said and to see everything else. Visual communication is just as important as auditory communication, and the two together paint the complete picture for you. It all comes down to effective communication skills.

> ***Your next adventure is waiting to be uncorked!***

Chapter Six

Be a Visionary

*A visionary is someone who lights
the way for the world.*

Throughout each chapter, thus far, we've talked about some of the most important core values of a true entre- preneur. We've learned that it takes strong self-belief, determination, curiosity, a stream of great questions, alignment with the universe, and a will to never give up on your dreams. When you take all of those core values and add them together, it is easy to see how this is the ultimate formula for success. What we're going to share with you next is what it looks like when we take all of those core values one step further and apply them to real life.

In the year 1787, the United States found herself in the early stages of infancy. Following a revolution from Great Britain, the states had freedom; however, our United States were not quite united just yet. The states had no way to enforce state lines, trade agreements, or even land agreements. It was during this time that a group of men met in a small room in Philadelphia and created the idea of a central federal government to solve the problems that the states were experiencing. This group of men started out with a blank slate, and they collaborated and came up with a system they believed would work. In order to put this central government in place, the men all agreed that the rights of the people would have to be protected. So, next, they set out to create protections for the rights of citizens. When everything was said and done, the men agreed upon ten amendments to our constitution and, today, this is what we know as the Bill of Rights. Something extraordinary happened that day—something that had never been done before—and it changed the course of history forever. From their experience of a lack of liberty, they laid the foundation for a new democracy. Their vision of freedom forever changed the world as we know it.

A visionary is someone who is capable of showing the world a brand-new way, enlightening the world and encouraging those around them to set out on an uncharted course and to explore the world around them with the single most important goal of changing it. *Webster* defines a visionary as "a person with original ideas about what the future will or could be like"—someone who can envision the future, a dreamer, who consistently remains ahead of the pack.

We have been lucky enough to study, and even know, a few truly inspiring visionaries: Thomas Edison gave us electricity, among other amazing inventions; The Beatles gave us music we simply couldn't live without—soundtracks to our memories; Steve Jobs created Apple and changed the way we use technology; and a visionary with whom you might not be familiar, Paul Fiore, forever changed the way we do our banking.

It has been said about Paul that he has the "Midas touch" when it comes to dealings in the financial industry. He is an investor, an advisor, a tremendously successful businessman, and one of the true visionaries of our time. Paul's philosophy on life is a rather simple one: you should always be looking forward to the future.

As a young man, Paul found himself to be curious about the problems of the world. He was always busy creating solutions, sometimes for problems only he could see. Paul graduated from New York University with a Bachelor of Science degree in Finance and Management, and the world wasn't ready for what he was about to bring to the table. What we're talking about is online banking—the capability to jump on your computer, and now your phone, and check your account balance, cleared items, pending items, and so on. Prior to this invention, the bank and mailed statements were really our only options for banking information. Being able to do our banking online changed everything. Imagine the hassle of having to go to the bank each time you needed to check whether or not an item had cleared, or recall the time spent balancing checkbooks and checking balances. The world of banking was due for an upgrade, and Paul set his sights high. He knew he would have his work cut out for him, but he was okay with the work. In fact, the work excited him because he understood the impact of what he was going to create for the masses.

When Digital Insight was born, it was 1995, and Paul had enlisted the efforts of his soon-to-be partner in business, Daniel Jacoby, to help start it. The duo saw what was coming down the pipeline with the creation of the Web browser and wanted to be some of the first people involved. In order to start their company, both men first had to leave their current positions. When Paul and Daniel approached their boss to let him know they would be leaving, he sent them out the door with best wishes and their very first investment. "Once I explained to the CEO what we were doing, he asked me how much we needed to get started. I told him we needed half a million dollars. He looked at me, thought about it for a second, and said, 'Anything worth doing for half a million dollars is worth doing for a million dollars,' and that's how we got our first investor."

At the young age of 24, Paul was already making a name for himself as one of the youngest CFOs in the history of the banking industry. By the age of 29, he had his first investor and was on his way to making banking history. All of the life skills we have talked about in this book thus far we can see in Paul's life. He was determined to succeed. He was not willing to let fear of failure stop him from pursuing something that had never been done before. He believed wholeheartedly in what he was doing. He knew he would have to work incredibly hard, and he accepted the challenge. Paul was ready to pave his own path and change the world, like a true visionary.

Just as those men in Philadelphia had set out to change the world, Paul would do the same. His first company, Digital Insight, was acquired by Intuit for over 1.35 billion dollars. From there he went on to create, invest, and leave his mark throughout the banking world in several different ways. He founded CU Wallet, a collaborative mobile wallet venture that is owned by credit unions. CU Wallet is designed to deliver white label products and services that enables credit unions to serve their members with their own branded mobile wallet. He also founded Double Beam, a mobile payment and cloud-based point-of-sale software venture that was recently acquired by a publicly traded firm.

Paul says he has been able to do this by getting out in front and anticipating the needs of the marketplace. He does this by always staying a few steps ahead of where the market is going next. When you are at the forefront of something new coming into the marketplace, you get to make the rules. You have the power to direct the influencers, who in turn direct the perception and the audience. The trickle-down effect is tremendous, and the visionary, who is at the forefront, chooses the direction the market will go.

There is a quote by Toba Beta that goes, "Visionaries build what dreamers have imagined." We want to take that even one step further and say that visionaries are dreamers with the capabilities to build everything they've imagined. Visionaries are problem solvers. They find themselves at the front of the pack because they are willing to tackle and solve problems most people wouldn't dream of taking on. Visionaries of Paul's magnitude are able to translate their visions into reality by identifying the path to get there and then taking action.

In the game of football, the quarterback is always looking downfield. He is not going to throw the football to the spot where the receiver is standing. The quarterback knows that he must be anticipating movement and where the receiver is moving to, and that's where the ball is thrown. Visionaries are never staring at a specific market, saying, "Where is this market?" The leader is asking, "Where is this market going?" And the true visionary is asking, "Where can I take this market?"

Anticipation of what is to come is the single best way to keep yourself ahead of the pack, no matter what field you are in. We live in a fast-paced, fast-changing economy. Change is always just right around the corner, and problems are always waiting to be solved. This is the work of a visionary—to tackle the eventual or potential problems of a market and apply that information to lead the market into future change.

> *Visionaries are true masters of change.*
> *They are not fearful of revolutions;*
> *they pursue them.*

One thing we know for sure is that change is a constant in our lives and in our businesses, and it will remain that way in the future. This can make things difficult if we are not prepared to deal with the change or if we find ourselves surprised or caught off guard. It is part of our conditioning and human nature to shy away from this change, or even problems. Avoidance doesn't do any good, but sometimes it feels safer than running full speed down the field and putting your belief in the fact that the ball will reach you. Life can be hard in that way, because we are taught avoidance more than we are taught anticipation, and this is something you are going to have to reprogram in your habits.

What would your life look like if, rather than running from problems, you reversed your approach and looked for problems to solve? What if, rather than working hard to avoid problems, you looked for problems to solve? This kind of proactive approach would certainly transfer across all areas of your life because you would be taking a strong leadership role in your future by essentially designing it. We know that anticipation is crucial to success, innovation, and remaining relevant in business. But we are also learning that these habits apply to every aspect of our lives. Everything benefits when we wake up and become strategic about where we are going and how we welcome (or shy away from) change.

Anticipation, over avoidance, allows you to see challenges, but this approach also allows you to see opportunities. The more you are looking, the more opportunity you will see. In chapter 1 we gave an example of what happens when you purchase a new car. Suddenly, after you've driven your vehicle off the lot, you begin to see "your" car everywhere. Your Reticular Activating System (RAS) is at work, and we can apply this same lesson to spotting opportunities as well as anticipating change. The more you seek out opportunity, the more opportunity you will find, and the more you anticipate change, the more change you will learn to anticipate.

Paul chose this path from a very young age, and it has paid off in tremendous ways. For Paul, the excitement of tackling problems is a unique experience, and one he has grown to love. His life reflects this, because just as soon as his current venture reaches maximum success, it seems he is onto the next big thing, making waves, and paving pathways. Every single time you grab your phone to check your account balance or make a deposit from the comfort of your home, we hope it inspires you to seek out your own problems to solve.

You have the abilities within you (remember the parable about the beggar and the gold?) to become a visionary for your time. Should you choose to accept the challenge, we've got some pointers to help you get there.

THE VISION

If you have the right vision, you should be able to jump right in and begin tackling what you believe will be the future of the market in which or the problem on which you are working. If your vision is not right, your best time spent will be on making sure you get it just right. If you want to be the leader of the pack, you first have to recognize the direction the pack is headed to successfully anticipate what the next steps will be. Refine, refine, refine. You'll know when your vision is just right, and only then should you begin taking steps forward.

EXPANSION

Once your vision is perfect, it is time to expand your vision and plan for the future. By adding layers to your vision, you are creating a plan for absolute success. Each layer should ultimately serve the purpose of moving you closer to achieving the vision you've laid out. If at any time throughout the process of expanding your vision, you realize the vision isn't right, this is the absolute best time to go back and tweak your vision. When the vision is right, the layers will fall into place seamlessly.

STRATEGIC PARTNERSHIPS

Paul knew the best engineer within XP Systems was Daniel Jacoby, and he partnered with Daniel because he knew their collaborative strength would be worth so much more than his singular effort. The saying "know your strengths; hire your weaknesses" holds a lot of merit. You may be forging new paths, but you don't want to lay the pavement alone. Know your strengths, and rely on your network for the strategic partnerships you will need to grow past the first layers of your vision.

REMOVING FRICTION

This applies to absolutely everything concerning your vision, your team, and anything else you can think of. The most successful visionaries have come up with solutions that remove friction in some way or another. Those men in Philadelphia were tasked with removing the friction from a country that was just learning to be a country. They accepted the challenge, and life as we know it is different because of their anticipation. For Paul, his technological movements have removed friction for users around the world by saving time, trips to the bank, and the hassles once associated with banking.

PERSISTENCE

It is said that Thomas Edison failed 10,000 times before he finally perfected the light bulb. Michael Jordan missed over 9,000 shots throughout his wildly successful basketball career. Walt Disney was told he lacked imagination. Every single person we have mentioned went on to find history-making success, and each legend, at one time or another, credited this truth to his or her persistence. If you can persevere, you will eventually get it right. If you never try, you most certainly will not.

ANTICIPATION OVER AVOIDANCE

Part of being a true visionary and strategic thinker is learning to anticipate rather than avoid, just as we've talked about in the beginning of this chapter. This is a habit that, once developed, will serve you well in so many aspects of your life. You learn to do this by asking yourself multiple times daily, "What can I contribute to this?" "Am I capable of solving this?" and "Are there changes I should be anticipating?" Taking time to tune in, as we've discussed in previous chapters, will bring about a higher level of awareness. You will find yourself feeling more tuned in to the universe, as well as life around you, just by developing the habit of asking yourself these questions. Remember, it takes time to secure a new habit in your life, so stick with it until you find yourself anticipating without the reminders.

Dr. Hill said it best: "Man is not bound by instinct; man is bound only by the imagination and the willpower of his own mind." Your visions are waiting; your future is in the balance.

Where will you go?

Chapter Seven

Surround Yourself with Good People

***If your table is full of winners,
the meal will satisfy your soul.***

The most intelligent people we've ever met in business and in life have a secret in common that we want to share with you. But before we do that, let us tell you a story...

There was a woman by the name of Alyssa, with whom we had the pleasure of doing business over several years' time. At a fairly young age, she was on track to do amazing things with her life. Not only was this go-getter motivated and aware, she was ultra-positive and a true beam of light to the people in her life. She had launched her own company by the age of 20, and business was steadily growing each year and even surpassing almost every round of quarterly goals set by the investors.

When she sat down to lunch one day, the overall mood was not the usual "pep rally" that our lunches typically were. It was obvious on Alyssa's face that something was wrong. There were stress lines that seemed new, and the smile Alyssa had that could light up entire rooms was missing. After our server took everyone's order and left us to catch up, we watched as she nervously bit her bottom lip, took a deep breath, and said, "I know you guys have never seen me like this. I am lost, and I am not sure where to go from here. My business is suffering, my personal life is suffering, and I don't know how to fix it." After at least 30 minutes of deep conversation, it came to light that Alyssa, who seemed to have everything with a life that was close to perfect, was being pulled under by energy vampires. No matter what she did to try to fix the unbalanced relationships in her life, it always ended up that she was giving so much and receiving nothing in return. Her entire life was suffering because of these lopsided connections, and it seemed like no matter what she did, she just couldn't escape.

We've all been there, right? We've all had at least one friend, partner, or business associate who takes until there is nothing left. Oftentimes, we don't even realize the effect this has on our energy and the rest of our life until the situation is dire and we are left with no other option but to take extreme action. One of the best-kept secrets to a sustained life of abundance is to surround yourself with others who are greater than you. Your closest friends and confidants should be exceptional, driven, and willing to push you toward success as well. We've all heard the saying, "You are the sum of the people you spend most of your time with." If this is true—that you are the sum of those surrounding you—perhaps it is time for you to take a very close look at what each of those people brings to the table. As Napoleon Hill so accurately pointed out, we should be seeking the company of people who influence us to think and act on building the life we so desire.

Without proper guidance, accountability, and support, we may find ourselves in a position of stagnation. Life can get away, and before you know it, five or ten years have gone by. When you are surrounded by truly exceptional people who are go-getters and seeking more out of life, you find yourself following suit. It is easy to chase dreams when everyone around you is chasing dreams. On the other hand, it is quite difficult to chase dreams when those around you aren't motivated enough to chase anything. There is a direct correlation between our choice of friends and our level of motivation.

Our friend Mark Ott is a great example of this life philosophy. When we met with Mark to interview him for this book, we took away something incredibly important about how he has found such tremendous success. You see, Mark is a firm believer in never being the smartest guy in the room. He works diligently to surround himself with unique, bright, and driven individuals who encourage him daily to be the best version of himself possible. By applying this philosophy to his life, Mark has accomplished some truly inspiring feats, and he has his eyes set on his biggest vision yet. We'll talk about that in a minute.

Mark is the founder of Ocean Aero, Inc., and serves as its chief technical officer. Ocean Aero has one, very hefty, goal: to change the world using the sun and wind to power new ideas in ocean exploration. Ocean Aero is founded on an extraordinary mix of ocean experience and world-class engineering innovation. From aerospace and aircraft carriers to record-breaking sail designs and space jumps, such expertise allows its team to take a fresh look at age-old ocean challenges. So back to Mark, whose biggest vision yet is coming to life right now—and that is to clean the oceans.

We've all heard about "Plastic Island" and the uncountable number of fragments and miniscule plastic pieces floating in our oceans. We've all seen the images of animals whose lives were lost, with their bodies flayed open to display a stomach full of plastic and garbage. The amount of plastics in our oceans, which is mostly discovered by trawling nets, is increasing every year. The danger in this is that there are so many unknowns. The truth is that we know there will be negative effects; we just don't know exactly what those will be, or how widespread.

For Mark, who does not call himself an environmentalist, this problem was one he felt Ocean Aero could tackle once his team completed most of the design aspects of FRED. FRED, which stands for Floating Robot for Eliminating Debris, is an unmanned, self-sustaining marine robot. By using solar and wind power, FRED is capable of collecting debris throughout our oceans 24 hours a day, year-round. This is an absolute game-changer for the marine robotics industry and, more importantly, for the health of our oceans.

As solar, sensor, and observational technologies advance, so does unmanned ocean vessel design. FRED represents a new class of autonomous, self-powered vessel design with both surface and subsurface versatility. Yes, you read that correctly—surface (above water) and subsurface (below water) versatility. FRED is a practical and efficient way to deploy and scale critical ocean observation and data collection as well, which means Ocean Aero is working hard to offer new ideas and options for efficiently accelerating ocean discovery. There are vast areas of our oceans where humans generally don't travel. The technology and vessels being created by Mark and his team at Ocean Aero can easily navigate those areas without putting human lives at risk.

Prior to the awesome work he is doing at Ocean Aero, Mark was the co-founder of Harbor Wing Technologies, where he managed and coordinated all aspects of design, engineering, and systems integration for a world-class technical team under contract to the U.S. Navy. The team's research and development led to the creation of the world's first wind-driven autonomous unmanned surface vessel. Under Mark's direction, the team at Harbor Wing Technologies successfully demonstrated to the Navy several iterations of these multi-hull, wingsail-driven designs. Mark is the co-creator and inventor on several U.S. patents inspired during the engineering process.

If you are as impressed as we are by Mark's story, surely you can understand why we set out to chat with him and figure out his secret to such a successful life. We knew there had to be a philosophy Mark was living daily, and we knew it would be powerful, because this much is evident just by looking at his life and his achievements thus far. What we were absolutely surprised to find was that for a man who had a vision to clean the oceans, he sure was humble and constantly lifting up those around him.

Throughout our conversation, we heard Mark repeat, time and time again, how lucky he was to have a marvelously qualified team supporting his efforts. He talked about how important it was to never be the brightest in the room and to surround yourself with truly extraordinary people, and how limitless your life becomes when you live this way. We have heard this theory before from some of the greatest minds of our time. Even Dr. Hill repeatedly pointed this out and coined the term "mastermind" as a way to identify a group of powerful people, as well as their collaborative power when each member's efforts were combined. He pointed out that not one individual person had enough education, abilities, and knowledge to ensure accumulation of great wealth, but with the cooperation of those around you—your mastermind group—the heights you could reach were immeasurable.

> ### *Work your strengths;*
> ### *hire your weaknesses.*

In previous chapters, we talked about working your strengths and hiring your weaknesses, and it is important to apply this philosophy to your everyday life. It is easier to become threatened by the abilities of others than it is to become humble and praising of their worth. During our interview, the casual way in which Mark shared with us that he worked hard to never be the smartest guy in the room was very telling of the kind of person he is. His ability to reach some amazing heights in his accomplishments, yet still remain incredibly humble and complimentary of those around him, says more than anything.

The people with whom you surround yourself have a huge impact on your life, and so does your environment. Your choices in life will place you either in a positive environment that is conducive to your growth or in just the opposite. Remember, you attract what you request from the universe. Ask yourself why successful people place themselves in the same environment with other like-minded individuals. It's because even the most successful people have weaknesses. They are human, just as we are. Being surrounded by other individuals on the same path or similar journeys helps them learn a little more about themselves from each other. That's why you may see an Elon Musk sharing the same table with a Beyoncé—successful but diverse personalities that may have something they can share with one another for growth.

There are three attributes in people that can identify them as good for you: they encourage you, they empower you, and they expand your horizons. You need people that support your dreams, visions, and ideas, goading you forward with encouragement and valuable contributions for your journey.

So, who are these good people, and where do you find them?

These people aren't special in any way, or at least they don't have to be. You aren't looking for the rich and famous to rub shoulders with to bolster your ego. These "good" people for whom you should be looking are invariably hiding in plain sight, among family members, friends, colleagues, or even casual acquaintances that you meet at the corner grocery store—all positive and happy people who will enrich your life.

"Good" does not mean the same thing for everyone, even though the broad, generalized parameters do give that impression. Every person is different. Things that make you happy don't necessarily work for us, and vice versa. Your ideas or vision may differ drastically from the next person, so you have to find the people who are "good" for you—those who align with your thoughts, temperament, and goals. This does not mean they have to be a clone of who you are, because that defeats the purpose. It has to be people who can understand where you are and your aspirations.

It isn't difficult to find these people if you're really looking for them. You have to be yourself and let them recognize you, just as you identify them.

Being surrounded by good people
is being surrounded by life.

When you are looking for these "good" people in your life, think of their qualities. Each of us may be looking for different things in a good person, but some of the common factors are:

- Are they positive?

- Do they have a happy disposition?

- How do their interactions with you affect you?

- Do they support you?

- Do they fill you with renewed energy?

If you can answer "yes" to most of these questions, those people are good for you.

Being with people whom you respect and like makes the emotional ride much easier and enjoyable. Your everyday life has you surrounded by all different kinds of people. Some are a joy to be with—their presence encourages and nurtures you—while others have the opposite effect and are caustic. These people drain you of energy and manipulate you through emotional bullying. These are what we have been referring to as "energy vampires." You must decide to refuse to be treated badly. Your well-being is influenced by those around you, and you must take charge of those whom you allow to enter your space. It's easy to talk about attracting "good people." It's much more difficult to talk about getting rid of the people who are a total drain on our lives.

At a subtler plane, energy is transferable, according to various Chinese and Hindu teachings. Sharing space with another person can result in sharing energy. Feelings are a part of that energy, and so moods and feelings are contagious. Being with a person who has a good disposition can keep your disposition on an even keel. This is the balance we have been talking about. The life story of each person has its highs and lows; there are choices you've made in which you take pride and decisions that you ruefully regret. These memories are reflections of the people we have had in our lives after having interacted with them on a daily basis. It is their actions and behaviors that resonate with your own to subconsciously influence your everyday choices. Choosing the people in your life is an important factor in how your life shapes up.

FORWARD MOMENTUM

It is challenging enough, in our crazy busy lives, to continue moving forward with continuous momentum. Being surrounded by strong, supportive individuals makes this task a lot easier because when you need it, you have their energy and example for a boost—just as you should be providing an example, as well as an energy boost, for those in your life when they need it. If you have surrounded yourself with what we refer to as "energy vampires," your life will fall out of balance fast and will remain that way until you do something to get back to that place of equilibrium.

Mark is a tremendous example of someone who leads a life of balance. This comes through in his work, his goals, and his energy when he talks about his vision for the future. It's no small feat to take on the task of cleaning the oceans. In fact, it almost sounds impossible. Except, with his remarkable team, Mark came up with a possible solution, and together, they are going after that seemingly impossible vision. We could use this opportunity to talk about dreams, and goals, life aspirations... but instead, let's call it what it really is—an exceptional team of people coming together to change the course of our future and the future of our oceans.

This proves to be a great example of what can happen when motivated minds gather together and set out to achieve their goals.

***Surround yourself with
who you want to be.***

Yes, there is definitely power in numbers...but those numbers have to equal something. If you are the sum of the people you spend the most time with and you strive to be a ten but they are all fives, they will bring down your average, and the only thing that produces is frustration and obstacles to achieving your success. Alyssa is a perfect example of how quickly people can bring down your house. At the end of our conversation, we urged her to start making changes so she could get her life back and find balance. Those changes aren't easy, which is why it's always a better option to be proactive. If you can look around the room and realize that you are bringing more to the table than anyone else, it's time for you to start seeking out more fulfilling relationships.

It's so easy to get stuck in a cycle of letting other people's energy ruin your own. We have all experienced this at some point or another in life. It's not to say those energy vampires are "bad," but they are just not a great fit for you and where you are in your life right now. It's okay to take a step back and conduct an honest assessment of where you actually are today and how that compares to where you would like to be.

As you contemplate deeply about the people with whom you interact, it becomes easier for you to identify the traits you are looking for and focus on filling your life with those who can help you cultivate positive and healthy relationships. In some situations it is not possible to choose these people. For example, at work you cannot choose your colleagues. But what you can do is look for those traits that can help you and concentrate on them. You can also share your positive traits that the other person may be looking for, making it a two-way relationship.

In your personal lives, barring immediate family, you can control the people with whom you choose to surround yourself. Assess the people you spend the most time with to see if they add constructively to, or subtract from, your life. Select your friends with care and caution because they create the environment in which you thrive. Give everyone an opportunity to be your friend, but only those who value your dreams and goals as much as you do should be made privy to them. If you have friends who sap your strength, you can tell them how you feel, or if you feel you may hurt their feelings, you can opt to spend less time with them.

The moment you are sincere with yourself about your own feelings, the more truthful you can be with others about how they make you feel. This will change your social life, bidding adieu to old friends, making new ones. But the decision to infuse this honesty into the way you want to live your life will bring about a transformation in your personality that will empower you with greater happiness.

Surrounding yourself with good people who have a positive temperament will clear the cobwebs of negativity that make a dungeon of your mind and create more room for nurturing good energy. It will enrich your life and encase you in a supportive and fertile environment, which fosters growth and understanding. But most of all, it will teach you to have the confidence to respect and love yourself.

This quote from Steve Maraboli sums it up perfectly: "If you hang out with chickens, you're going to cluck, and if you hang out with eagles, you're going to fly."

Mark has spent time as a competitive sailor and as a boat designer. He has worked with huge corporations and even our Navy to create solutions to problems most of us go our entire lives without even thinking about. Let Mark's story be an inspiration to your life. He has a vision to clean the oceans, and he is actually doing it. There is nothing more inspirational than that. This is an amazing story, and Mark's philosophy can easily be applied to your life. That alone should be reason enough for you to be motivated to action.

This is Mark's magic key to success.

Catch that wave and ride it all the way in.

Chapter Eight

Perfection from Imperfection

Your imperfections are your perfections.

The people with whom you associate will impact your success and happiness. Success is not an independent sport—it's a collaborative effort that benefits greatly from the partnerships and associations with people who can help you make things happen faster than you can alone. Not only do you benefit from the experience and knowledge these people have accrued, but through them you have access to the knowledge and experience of the people who have influenced them through the years. Even better, your connection with people provides you with a direct connection to the people in their entire network. In essence, your own network can be extensive, even endless, through the people you know and associate with often.

The greatest achievements in history were the result of a team effort. Our nation had more than one Founding Father, and our Declaration of Independence was signed by 56 delegates. There is power in numbers, but there is a greater power when we tap into our network and connections to make things happen. The people we know can be the key to something magnificent and beautiful in our lives.

Knowing that, we set out to find someone who makes things happen on a grand scale—a get-it-done person who could share what it takes to turn influence into results. Our quest led us to an impressive entrepreneur who goes by a memorable and unique name, Ugly Sims.

Steve Sims is the founder and owner of The Bluefish, the world's leading luxury concierge firm. Through an extensive network, Steve provides the highest level of personalized experiences and cutting-edge entertainment to his clients, which include celebrities, professional athletes, corporate executives, and a unique class of individuals who strive to live life to its fullest.

If it's on your bucket list, Steve will deliver it. He's the force behind amazing experiences that would appear to be seemingly impossible. His clients have become James Bond in Monte Carlo; they've boarded a submarine for a trip to the Titanic, received cooking lessons from world-class chefs, jammed with celebrity recording artists, received private backstage concerts, and even had walk-on roles on hit television shows.

But if you ask Steve what it is he does, he'll tell you, "I make things happen. I get people to do what they dream and desire by using my contacts and connections to pull it off."

Fascinated, we were curious how one attains that level of influence. What does it take to be able to open opportunities and acquire access to prestigious people and experiences? Most of all, we knew it takes a special personality to make things happen at such an ultimate level, so we wanted to find just what makes Steve Sims tick.

Steve explained that this wasn't something he just fell into—he's been doing the seemingly impossible all of his life. Since he was a little kid, he's wanted to get into places he wasn't supposed to be in and do things he wasn't supposed to do. His uncanny ability to do just that grew into an art that he's perfected over the years. In 1994, he began using his talents to get people into elite and VIP events in Asia. Today, he's in Los Angeles, California, where he's hosted Elton John and other music superstars, tech geniuses, and the man who would become our 45th president, Donald Trump.

Steve Sims is the poster child of "if there's a will, there's a way." He has mastered the art of cutting through the degrees of separation to find the one connection that can make anything happen. And he does it without sugarcoating his requests—an angle that gave birth to his nickname, Ugly Sims.

"Most of the time, it's fascinating. I'm constantly baffled as to who I'm meeting and who I bump into. My angle is ugliness...I'm not referring to my stunning good looks, though some might think so. Rather, I've built a reputation of being a can-do man, but I've also built a reputation of being very raw, transparent, and ugly. Quite simply, though, I'm incredibly easy to understand."

In other words, Steve cuts to the chase and gets to the point—at lightning speed. Forget flowery compliments and unnecessary verbiage—Steve achieves the seemingly impossible because he lets everyone know who he is and what he wants up front. He hides nothing, exposing the good, the bad, and the ugly to make things happen.

"I have a direct policy. When I talk to people, I tell them what I need and ask how I can make it happen. It makes it impossible for people to misunderstand what I want. It's refreshing. When I communicate with people, whether the person is the head of the Oscars, the Vatican, or NASA, I need to be an incredible master communicator and let them quickly know what I want, what's in it for them, and why it would be good for them to do it."

Steve explained that this level of frankness is not new, but it has become a lost art. While technology has made it faster and easier to communicate, people take too long to get to the point. One reason for that is that we've become numb and suspicious when people communicate with us. We don't trust our allies and have adopted the principle of "if it sounds too good to be true, it probably is."

Steve provides experiences that can fit that description. While they may seem to be too good to be true, he assures us that they are not. It is through his extensive network and the connections he's made throughout the years that he turns dreams into reality. Who he knows is a big part of the equation, but Steve attributes an equal portion of his success to knowing how to communicate with those connections.

"When people communicate quickly, succinctly, and are to the point, they cut through the noise. Pre-laptop, pre-iPad, and pre-technology boomers understand this. Prior to the tech boom, we were direct and to the point. Today, everything is filtered. We filter our responses and requests.

"Some people call this directness being ugly. However, the byproduct of that attitude is people know who you are because you are not hiding behind any flowery grammar or over-embellished wording. They know your tone, who you are, and what you're after. That builds relationships, which people don't know how to do."

By being "ugly" and saying it like it is, no holds barred, Steve has earned a reputation for being raw. What you see is what you get, and he's not ashamed of it. In fact, it's precisely how he's leveraged this self-proclaimed "imperfection" into a perfection. What he's done is perfected the art of using a perceived fault to his benefit. The problem is, he states, that the majority of people hide their imperfections and faults, rather than embracing them. In other words, we worry so much about our image that we don't allow ourselves to be who we truly are.

"As people get richer, others distance themselves from them and treat them differently. You treat someone who is a billion-aire differently than someone who is struggling to pay their mortgage. There is an image for everything. We are bombarded with imagery, whether it is social feed or magazines. Every picture can be filtered. If you take a beautiful picture of your family on the beach, before it's posted on social media you edit that picture, enhancing the image to make it prettier before anyone else sees it. We've become numb now to what is fact and raw imagery, raw talk, and raw conversation."

Raw conversation in Steve's world means being upfront and getting to the point without wasting a second. It's about being direct, which some might interpret as being blunt. By capitalizing on his unusual style, he proves that sometimes all we need to do to get what we want is to come right out and ask for it. It's a style of communication that can be perceived as harsh, but it's precisely how Ugly Sims has distinguished himself as a master communicator, which turned him into a remarkably successful entrepreneur.

What Steve has really done is leverage the principle of instant gratification. Our information-rich society wants answers...and we want them now. If we have a question, we can send a text and get an immediate response. We can even ask Siri or Alexa what we need to know and get the answer we're seeking quickly. Steve's directness caters to people's need for instant gratification because he tells them what he wants and what they need to know before they have a chance to question his motives.

Some may deem Steve's communication style as ugly, designating it an imperfection or a flaw. But it is that very style that has earned Steve notoriety and respect among both his clients and his vast network. By removing the smoke and mirrors from his delivery and presentation, Steve has eliminated the possibility of being misconstrued or misunderstood.

Steve told us that there is a difference between being an effective communicator and a good persuader. "Brian Kurtz and Joe Polish once said that there is a difference between being easy to understand and impossible to misunderstand. I'm impossible to misunderstand. You cannot confuse me with anyone or misinterpret my motives, thoughts, feelings, emotions, or actions after I respond to any question. Respect grows from that. Respect grows when you remove your filter and get to the point—be who you say you are."

Dare to be yourself. Be unique—flaunt your faults, embrace them, and turn them into assets. It is in your uniqueness that you have the power to influence and persuade others, but first they need to know precisely what it is you want and that your motives are sincere. It's a communication style that revolves around candor and honesty, and one that Steve credits with his fast track to success. It's how he gets things done...and how he gets people to help him get those things done, even if they're seemingly impossible. Here's how you can do the same:

1. **State the purpose of your communication immediately.** When communicating with others, especially when you're soliciting their participation or cooperation, tell them quickly what you want. Too often, people misconstrue what is being asked of them because it gets lost or watered down.

2. **Avoid excess verbiage.** Not only does this indicate that you respect the other person's time, but by being clear and concise, they won't question your motives. Eliminate lengthy introductions and explanations; instead, state in as few words as possible what you want.

3. **Let them know what's in it for them.** People do want to help others, but they also want to know that their efforts, time, and/or money are appreciated. Make it clear how they will benefit by agreeing to your request.

4. **Be authentic.** People can and will notice when people misrepresent who they are or what they want. By exposing your true self, in both your words and actions, you will earn their respect and trust, two ingredients necessary to build relationships.

Steve has built a world-class business around respect, trust, and authenticity. Being "ugly and raw" is his claim to fame, but when we met Steve, we quickly realized that there were no layers of the onion to peel away before we could get a glimpse into who he is and the magic key to his success. It took no time at all to realize that his perfection was in his so-called imperfection, and through it he has created an engaging brand, one that attracts people to him and makes them want to help him. And that's a thing of beauty.

> *Be yourself—it's the one thing you can do better than anyone else.*

Chapter Nine

Find Your Uniqueness

Do the best you can do…
in all that you do.

As shown in many of these stories, there is a learning curve to success. There are different levels and kinds of learning. Brian Sidorsky had to learn how to learn. But there are some who have to learn specific things, such as a new language. Others might walk into a totally new environment—they have to learn their community or a new country. Just like leaving home and walking onto a college campus for the first time, the world is full of unknowns and new experiences that require us to put on our learning caps.

Makarand (Mak) Jawadekar is no stranger to strange people, places, or things. Mak was a young 25-year-old when he migrated from India to the United States. Alone and in a foreign country, he had to adapt to just about everything he encountered. Mak admits it wasn't without challenges.

"I was young and had never left my home country. The temperature in India was always warm, between 70 and 100 degrees.

Going from India to Minnesota was like walking into a refrigerator. It was extremely cold, and I had never seen snow before—it was quite different. So was the culture, and I had to get used to that. The third challenge was being alone. I no longer had a family structure. In India, a large family structure was in place, and we didn't have to worry about getting from one place to another. Now, I had to help myself—I had to learn to drive for the first time. I also had to get used to doing my own cooking, which was something I'd never done before."

Imagine being in a foreign land where you don't know a soul. A college campus is an adjustment for anyone, but it was quite a culture shock for Mak. The educational system is different in the United States, and so are the people. Not only did he have to adapt to those things, but he also had to obtain employment in order to support himself. Within a week, he found a job.

That job was the first of his impressive career. Mak's name might not be a household name that is familiar to you, but his accomplishments probably are. For nearly three decades, Mak served as Director of Portfolio Management and Performance at Pfizer Global Research and Development. At Pfizer, he was instrumental in creating the antibiotic Zithromax and Zoloft, an antidepressant drug. Retired, he is still active in the pharmaceutical industry and currently serves on several companies' advisory boards and also consults with biotechnology/pharmaceutical companies for global outreach in emerging market regions.

Undoubtedly, Mak has had an impressive career, and he places the credit for his successes on his work ethic, which he applied to everything—his studies, his work, and his relationships. "From the time I started classes at the University of Minnesota to get my

PhD in pharmaceutics to today, it is my work ethic that helped me excel. I studied hard, and I played hard. Whatever I did, I put 100 percent into it. That helped me complete my doctorate and also earned me some accolades from the university to get into the next phase of my life, where I could contribute for the betterment of human health. That's where I knew I could make a difference."

Mak states he got his strong work ethic due to his family background and the influence of his father, who taught him to be humble and that he shouldn't say no to anything unless the challenge would totally consume him. He goes on to state that there is never anything in the world that can totally consume him.

"I had very humble beginnings. My father worked for the government in India. When I was 25, I came to the United States. Obviously, I didn't know anybody. I had to learn a lot. My success is due to hard work and concerted effort. Once I set a goal, I had to do everything to achieve that goal. Along the way, I learned I had to have a strong Rolodex. Having the right people on your side—the right people to talk to and take advice from—helped me quite a bit. I created a wonderful network of people who were experts in their field. People in other sectors who were doing one thing already taught me how we could apply those sectors to pharmaceuticals. That accelerated our results, which is important in pharmaceuticals because you have to be in the forefront.

"In my life to date, I have learned a lot. My advice to others is to keep your network alive. By yourself, you can do only so much, but if you learn to take advice from friends and experts, you won't waste your time reinventing the wheel. People have been there and done that. Find the mentor and network to help you. That will put you ahead of the game, and you'll not only save time in achieving your goals, but you'll be almost 100 percent assured of achieving success."

Formulating a new drug can be quite challenging. With Zoloft, the specific challenge was the formulation because of the physical properties of the active ingredient and how it could be formulated into a pill or tablet. Mak had to utilize all of his scientific expertise to make it happen.

It didn't happen overnight. Not only did it require Mak's expertise, but it required a leap of faith that it could be done. That faith, combined with his work ethic, is embedded in everything he has done, from the time he left his family and country in pursuit of an education and a career to the moment he developed the right formulation of a billion-dollar drug. Mak describes that faith and how it impacted his success:

"The first leap of faith I undertook when I came to the States was doing my job and doing the best I could. Having that full confidence in myself led me to work and chisel at creating my dreams. Then the sky was the limit. There were times I felt that I was walking on water. I felt I could accomplish any challenge that was thrown at me."

Let's look at Mak's road map to success:

1. **Have a strong work ethic.** Giving it his all has always been Mak's mantra. Whether he was studying or working his way through college, he treated each endeavor as if it was the most important thing and something that had to be done

right. Doing even simple things well is a standard of excellence that will influence your outcome.

2. **Have faith.** If you don't believe you can do something, you probably can't. It takes confidence to tackle difficult or complex ambitions, but that confidence is precisely what will see it through to fruition.

3. **Have a strong network.** Not only do you need a strong network, but you need to keep it alive. It is the relationships that you nurture that will be of mutual benefit to all parties. Choose people who are more experienced than you, learn from them, and apply that education into your sector.

Mak reminded us that while it is critical that the right people are in your Rolodex, you have to provide value to them, as well. "I also recognize that you have to have something that brings people to you. Understanding what is unique in you is the question. If you can find that uniqueness, you can move mountains. I utilized that uniqueness in me and then gave those golden nuggets to other people, and we were able to accomplish even more. Having the right people to connect to will help you connect the dots. That is the real key—if you help someone achieve something, that is a feather in your cap. If they succeed, it is a key to your happiness."

Mak spent his career, and now his retirement, contributing to others. While working at Pfizer, he was clearly instrumental in the development of pharmaceuticals that improve lives. His contributions to the public and pharmaceutical industry are a testament to his work ethic and principles. Giving it his all, he's built credentials that have made him highly valuable as an advisor across the globe.

*Do simple things well...*it's Major League Baseball manager Joe Maddon's philosophy. It brought the Chicago Cubs a World Series championship after a 108-year drought. It brought Mak from being a young immigrant in a foreign country to becoming the inventor of medicines like Zoloft and Zithromax. What can it do for you?

Do simple things well.

Chapter Ten

Know the Track

I live to work…not work to live.

Mak Jawadekar loved what he did so much that he's still active in the pharmaceutical industry. Retired since 2010, he's spent the last eight years serving on advisory boards and is actively involved in the pharmaceutical industry. It takes more than a desire to "keep busy" to choose to continue such a level of involvement—it takes a love for what you do. In fact, there are some who choose to continue their careers well beyond retirement age. You might recognize the names of these musicians who were still stepping onto stages and into recording studios after passing the 70-year milestone: Mick Jagger, Tony Bennett, Brian Wilson, Paul McCartney, and Bob Dylan.

Their careers and lives are inseparable for those musicians. What they do is part of who they are, so they chose to continue performing, even if they didn't have to. We wondered what the secret was to such a lifelong devotion and satisfaction, and we found just the person to drive the point home.

Bob Bondurant was a professional racer. If it had wheels, he likely raced it. At the age of 18, he was racing Indian motorcycles on dirt tracks in Los Angeles. Sports cars soon followed. In 1959, Bob won the West Coast "B" Production Championship and received the Corvette Driver of the Year Award. Between 1960 and 1963, he competed in 32 races, winning an impressive 30 of them.

In 1963, he won the Grand Prix of Riverside, and in both 1964 and 1965 Bob won the GT class at the 24 Hours of LeMans. His claim to fame includes winning seven out of ten FIA World Championship races, among other notable accomplishments.

It wasn't long before Bob's successes caught the attention of Ferrari, who asked him to debut its Formula One team at the Watkins Glen Grand Prix. Hollywood even took note and hired Bondurant to be a driving consultant for the film *Grand Prix*, which starred James Garner.

An accident ended Bob's impressive racing career. Doing 150 miles per hour, a steering arm broke, causing Bob's car to flip eight times. Suffering injuries to his legs, back, ribs, and feet, doctors told Bob that it was unlikely he'd ever walk again.

He proved them wrong. Back on his feet, he had to determine what he was going to do with his life. It was in his hospital bed that he had an epiphany—he'd enjoyed teaching actors the art of driving—why not open a driving school? On Valentine's Day in 1968, he opened the Bondurant Driving School.

It wasn't an overnight sensation. There were only three students in his first class. The next class had even fewer: two students attended, but they weren't just any students—Bob's class consisted of actors Robert Wagner and Paul Newman, who, like

James Garner, were training for a role in a film. As his school grew, it received recognition, as well as support from companies like Ford Motor Company, which offered to provide Bob with vehicles for his school.

Today, Bob owns a purpose-built driver-training facility that maintains more than 200 vehicles, sedans, SUVs, and open-wheel cars, all race prepared. Bob is in his eighties, and not only does he teach, but Bob also races in vintage races. His fascinating career made him the perfect person to shed light on what it takes to attain such a long and fulfilling lifetime of achievement.

"I live to work...not work to live." When you love what you do, it is not working. Actively teaching and racing, Bob always has a smile on his face that is proof that he's loving every minute of it. Loving what you do isn't a requirement for a career, but it certainly is an advantage. People who love their careers are more motivated, productive, and fulfilled. They enjoy better mental health, and by some accounts, better physical health. It's also said that they are more effective leaders and teachers.

Bob Bondurant loves to race, which is why he is the master teacher to more than 300,000 graduates since his school opened its doors in 1968. Turning a career- and life-changing setback into a success is not an easy feat, so we asked Bob if he ever had any doubts.

"I thought, 'Damn, what am I going to do now? ...Maybe I'll do a school. I have to make a living somehow, and if I can't walk, I need to be doing something.' For about two or three days, I wrote down on a legal pad how I would do the school—the cars, the parts to do a school, everything I could think of. I needed sponsors. So I put it away and didn't look at it for a little while."

The idea stuck with him, and that legal pad didn't stay tucked away for long. As soon as Bob overcame his injuries, he launched his plan. He credits his ability to do both to having a positive mental attitude. Instead of lamenting about his injuries or the end to a rich, rewarding, and much-loved career, he chose to continue doing what he loved, just in another way.

The philosophies Bob applied to his success behind the wheel and around the track were the philosophies he used in creating and growing his school. We asked Bob what it takes to be recognized as a top performer. His answer was enlightening.

"Know the Track." Practice pays off. When practicing for races, Bob would drive the course over and over until it was no longer new to him. "We were there to learn the circuit well so we had a chance to win the race." In any business, you have to know your product, service, and customer well—you have to know how it is different from or better than another. The more you practice and learn, the better you will be in delivering a performance or a service that is commendable. It's the pursuit of champions—and you must know the track like you're a champion.

Then Bob shared another philosophy that he practiced and teaches to this day.

"Always look where you want to go." You cannot drive a straight line if you're not looking ahead. If you're skiing downhill, you have to look ahead or you'll fall. The same is true in any business—you cannot get where you want to go unless you're looking in that direction. You have to keep your eyes one step ahead of the curve in order to be able to maintain a steady pace throughout that curve.

Looking where you want to go has another benefit. It will reveal any obstacles or risks in your path. This will give you sufficient time to make a necessary adjustment or maneuver to prevent you from encountering something that could slow you down, or worse—require that you pull over and back out of the race.

It's the concept of keeping your eye on the prize, whether that's rounding the next phase or curve or attaining the end goal—the coveted trophy for which you've worked hard.

Without a doubt, Bob knows race tracks, and he knows the track to success. It's a labor of love that he doesn't think of as work—it's simply living what he loves. His philosophy has rewarded him with a long career that began when racing was more of a pastime enjoyed by a small segment and has continued into today, where racing is a sport that has grown exponentially and attracted millions of fans since the day he opened his school. While you might not see Bob behind the wheel, he's the man behind many of the drivers you see on the circuit and on the silver screen. At 80-plus years, he's still the champion to beat.

Always look where you want to go.

Chapter Eleven

Constant Forward Motion

Progress is not linear.
It's exponential growth.

It was 1968 when Bob Bondurant opened his driving school. Let's fast-forward two decades. The year is 1988, the Beach Boys are making serious waves on the music scene, you can purchase an Amiga computer with a color monitor for a mere $849.00, and NASA has just launched the Hubble Telescope deep into space for exploration. There was a lot going on in 1988, especially with NASA. This is the same year NASA decided to resume its space shuttle program, only two and a half years after the Challenger disaster took the lives of seven astronauts. As NASA set out to once again change the course of history, its forward momentum didn't go unnoticed. Walter O'Brien was just 13 years old at the time, and he was fascinated with the space shuttle program. He hacked into NASA's databases, stole a copy of the shuttle blueprint, printed it out, and hung it on his bedroom wall. Imagine his surprise when all those black cars showed up outside his house looking for "the hacker." His life story only gets more interesting from there.

"When I was 13, I thought I was pretty hot stuff because I knew BASIC programming, self-taught on the family's Commodore 64. One of my crowning accomplishments was writing a silly little program that showed a crudely drawn space shuttle lifting off in a cloud of pixelated smoke."

We've discussed visionaries, and Walter is a true visionary—a futurist. His mind comprehends and dissects what is happening around him at lightning-fast speed, and he uses that information to understand what the future will hold for the human race...but that's just in his free time. His day job is much more intense and complex. His company, Scorpion Computer Services, is one of the world's leading experts in the application of computer science and artificial intelligence. His technology, intelligence, and security services have saved lives in corners of the world most of us have never even heard of, and oftentimes it is Walter himself, at his computer for days and sleepless nights on end, who is making sure everything happens as it should. He is manning the computer rather than the machine gun, and his role in these operations, around the world, is saving numerous lives.

The year 1988 is also when Walter launched Scorpion Computer Services. If anyone was capable of launching a security business at the age of 13, it was Walter. By the age of 9, he was designated a child prodigy after scoring 197 on an IQ test administered by one of his teachers. At 16, he ranked first in Irish national high-speed computer problem-solving competitions. At 18, he competed in the World Olympics in Informatics and has ranked as high as the sixth-fastest programmer in the world. His childhood and young accomplishments are impressive. Even his degree, Bachelor of Science in Computer Science and Artificial Intelligence with honors from Sussex University in the United Kingdom, is impressive. Walter had accomplished more by the age of 18 than most accomplish in their entire adult lives, and he didn't stop there. The list just goes on.

The U.S. Department of Homeland Security certified his business, Scorpion, as being of national interest to the United States economy and granted Walter an "Extraordinary Ability" EB 1-1 Visa (also granted to Albert Einstein and Winston Churchill). He is a frequent public speaker for IEEE (Institute of Electrical and Electronics Engineers) and teaches as a mentor with the Founder Institute, the world's largest idea-stage incubator. He has worked with the world's largest mutual fund company, as well as Fujitsu, Microsoft-Trados, Oracle Corporation, Baltimore Technologies, and Critical Path. Walter serves as chairman for Houston Technology Center, Strike Force Solutions, Talentorum Alliance, and Lawloop. It's a blessing that he doesn't need much sleep at night, because we aren't sure when he even has time left *to* sleep.

If all of that isn't enough, CBS decided to turn Walter's life into a television drama, which Walter helps direct. The show is aptly named Scorpion, which also happens to be Walter's hacker name. Stories inspired by reality are the best kind, and certainly truth is always more intriguing than fiction. When CBS decided to create Scorpion and model it after this self-described computer genius, the skeptics came out in droves. With any great accomplishment comes major responsibility and, at the very least, a few haters. For Walter, working in a space that is oftentimes top secret, undercover, and mostly classified leaves little room for bragging. There are no medals or certificates to hang on the wall. So Walter must simply smile at his haters and the skeptics out there while they attempt to diminish his story.

After learning about Walter's life and seeing his amazing list of accomplishments, we knew there had to be something specific he was doing, some sort of philosophy he was applying, to be leading such an incredible life. What we learned is something obvious to the way Walter lives his life, if you take a close look. Walter lives by the philosophy of remaining in constant forward motion, focusing intensive efforts on the task at hand for several years to reach expert level.

During our interview, Walter said to us, "Progress is not linear. It's exponential growth." If we break that down, what he's really saying is that as we accelerate forward, growth becomes more and more rapid, rather than just growing the same amount every day or every week. Progress is *not* linear and thank goodness for that. Yes, slow and steady wins the race...but in our fast-paced world, rapid growth is the key to finding success in a major way. If we apply Walter's theory to his own life, we can see something incredible happening. With each passing year, Walter's growth is so tremendous that it falls off the chart. There is absolutely something to be said for working on something significant over a long period of time with consistent and extreme focus.

This can be worrisome in a world where, according to a 2015 report by Microsoft, we are bringing up new generations with the attention span of, on average, 8 seconds. In the year 2000, that number was 12 seconds, which means we now have an attention span that is less than that of a goldfish. In order to be capable of applying extreme focus for long periods of time, you are going to have to train your mind to cooperate.

IMPACT EVOLUTION

We can see how true it is that growth is exponential, especially when we apply this theory to the evolution of the human race. Our growth, on a whole level, is speeding up as we evolve, and the only thing slowing that growth down is our adoption curve. The adoption curve is how long it takes us to adopt, accept, or warm up to new growth, ideas, and changes. Humans tend to resist change, and this slows down our adoption curve quite a bit.

We are skeptical by nature, and we use this built-in system for defense against change that might challenge our everyday, normal lives. Our minds are working overtime to question every last little bit of change to make sure we won't be forced to change or sacrifice our comfort in return for this possible new growth. Variation is scary because it forces us into a state of consciousness by interfering with autonomy, pushing us to give up a certain level of control. A lack of control turns into fear, which brings on our defense system, resistance, and sometimes even the "fight or flight" response.

As this resistance to change is taking place, there is actually more going on below the surface of which you might not even be aware. You see, as you are trying to decide whether or not the change that is about to take place, or that is taking place, is acceptable change, your mind is working on an entirely different aspect of the situation. Change always relates back to the person because this is what we do as human beings.

***We make everything personal to where we
are in life at any given moment.***

As we are making the change personal and relating it to our lives, what our brains are actually trying to figure out is whether or not this change will challenge our power. For example, "If I accept X Technology, will I be able to keep up? Will my skill level be enough or will I become obsolete?"

Uber is a great example of this. When Uber first came out, the naysayers came out in full force. They were angry, they wanted to tell you every single reason why Uber wasn't going to work, and they wanted Uber shut down. The loudest people shouting were the ones who stood to lose profit and power because of Uber, and they were (perhaps) especially mad that they didn't think of the idea themselves. Take a look at Uber today. This is a company that has worked its way into our lives. Everyone knows who they are, and they have become a viable and reliable trans-portation option.

The amount of time it took us, from the moment Uber became public, to the time we stopped doubting its viability, is our adop-tion curve. In this specific case, the curve was less than seven years. If you look back in history, you will see that this curve time is becoming shorter and shorter as our growth and evolution accelerates (exponentially).

As our adoption curve becomes less and less, our willingness to focus and see things through has to become greater for us to remain competitive in the world and even in our own lives. Our success will depend on this application of time and effort. Knowing what we know about the avoidance of change, it is clear that we truly are creatures of habit. This is something we can use to our advantage—to create daily habits that will assist us in long-term focus and determination. In chapter 1, we learned about John Assaraf's conclusion that it takes 56 days to cement a habit into our lives. If we can use this knowledge to create habits that will assist us in accomplishing long-term goals, our success growth will also become exponential.

> *Aristotle taught us, "We are what we*
> *repeatedly do. Excellence therefore, is*
> *not an act, but a habit."*

HABIT BUILDING

The process of building habits into our lives is not easy. If it were, everyone would do it, and everyone would accomplish their dreams and the goals they set out for themselves. It is a simple process to plan to build habits into our lives, but it isn't easy to follow through, so let's approach that topic next.

There are now decades of research and scientific evidence on self-discipline, motivation, and habit building. Based on all of this research and evidence, we know that there are very specific steps you need to take to successfully incorporate habits into your life to help you achieve your goals. Let's start with these steps:

1. **Eliminate distractions:** We have talked about the burden of distractions in our busy, noisy world. They will easily pull you from your goals if you allow it to happen.

2. **Eliminate naysayers:** Nothing will derail you faster than someone working hard to rain on your parade. We feed off the energy of those around us, and if the energy is negative and constantly bringing you down, you will never find success. The people around you are as important as the goals you set because they have the potential to help you rise up or watch you continuously fall down.

3. **Go big, and then go small:** Your "big picture goal" is made up of several small pieces, just like a puzzle. Once you've realized the big picture goal, it's time to break it up into small achievable steps (puzzle pieces) that are working to move you closer to achieving your master plan of greatness.

4. **Make a plan:** Daily quotas are a necessary part of the path to your success. A quota is a proportional part of your total... in other words, small pieces of your big picture. Your daily quota is the minimum amount of work you have to accomplish each day to make achieving your "big picture goal" a reality.

5. **Use the 3 R's system for habit formation:** These are *reminder*, *routine*, and *reward*, and each one works with the others to help cement habits into your life.

    a. **Reminder:** If you want to cultivate a new habit or improve an old one, you must first work on reminding yourself to do the routine regularly. Most people will try to convince you that the crux of forming a new routine (and then habit) is all about self-control and willpower. This couldn't be further from the truth. You must set up a trigger, initially, to help you build the routine.

    b. **Routine:** This is you taking action, following your reminder, and following through.

    c. **Reward:** The reward is how your new habit or routine benefits you. Maybe you are happier, in better shape, or more organized. Whatever that reward may be, it will work as your encouragement to continue with your habit building.

Your life is the sum of your habits. Your happiness is a result of your habits. Your level of success is a result of your habits. Your level of fitness is also a result of your habits. Ultimately, what you do repeatedly goes into shaping the person you become, governs the things you believe, and etches out the personality you project. Behavioral psychology research has proven that these set patterns and processes cultivate habits.

IMPLEMENTATION INTENTIONS

All of those steps are great, but if you have no way of implementing the habits and quotas you come up with, then you are stuck where you started. Implementation Intentions is a strategy that will help you reach your goals through intentionality and consistency.

Implementation Intentions works by picking a regular part of your schedule or day and attaching another "link in the chain" to a habit you've already established. Let us give you an example. Let's say every day you go into work and get coffee and your mail before heading to your desk. This is your routine every single day. You've decided you would like to begin maintaining a more organized workspace. To use the process of Implementation Intentions, you would say, "When I get into the office, I am going to grab my coffee, grab my mail, and then organize my desk." You are building a new habit into your already existing habits.

Science is showing us, time and time again, that these contextual cues actually work. This strategy, when applied, allows you to self-regulate, which will lead to better overall goal attainment and increased behavior and habit modification. In simpler terms: this strategy puts you in control of your own destiny, as well as the steps you'll take to reach your big picture goal.

When you say, "I want to have a more organized workspace; I'm going to clean it more often," you haven't created any clear, actionable steps to help get you there, and this is a major reason why people fail to achieve their goals. They have an idea of what they want but no clear way to make it happen in their lives. Remember, we are creatures of habit. By building our goal steps into our lives in the form of new habits attached to existing habits, our chances at success go up tremendously.

Once you've created a clear and concise plan mentally, your goal and the steps necessary to achieve it become solidified and automatic. This leads to better attention, memory, and perception of the entire big picture, as well as the small steps you will take to get what you want. When you take the guesswork out and the steps become clear and automatic, the steps no longer require conscious effort, which means your brain stops recognizing the step as change and, in turn, stops resisting the behavior.

In chapter 2, we talked about big-picture goals. Write them down, along with your "why," and carry them with you as a daily reminder. This helps when you feel that you may be getting off track. If you can keep your "why" at the center of your day, your chances at success will double.

> ***Choose your habits prudently, because,***
> ***as John Dryden astutely stated—***
> ***"We first make our habits,***
> ***then our habits make us."***

As soon as you've realized your big-picture goals and have taken the steps outlined above, you will be on the path to finding the abundant life you seek. The only thing capable of stopping you *is you*. Your level of discipline and the amount of effort you are willing to apply will decide the outcome of your life, your success, and your ability to achieve your big-picture goals.

Anything done repeatedly over a long period of time forms a habit. Doing something significant once is relatively easy; we've all done it. Supporting a good cause at work, helping out at a walk-a-thon, giving to the needy...but sustaining those actions over a period of time is always difficult. The only way this can be done effectively is by creating a routine. The conscious repetitive actions in a routine can set you into a rhythm, which can become a habit if it endures. We really aren't strangers to routine. Though we may resist it at first, when we consciously structure habits and routine into our lives, they instantly become better.

At the age of 26, Winston Churchill was thrilled to leave the military because he wished to "be free of discipline and authority, and set up perfect independence in England with nobody to give me orders or arouse me by bell or trumpet." Except, he never did away with his daily schedule or routine; he just created a routine he enjoyed and stuck with it. We have great insight into this from a researcher who visited Churchill while helping him write his books who said, "He was totally organized, almost like a clock. His routine was absolutely dictatorial. He set himself a ruthless timetable every day and would get very agitated, even cross, if it was broken."

We are told that it takes 56 days to cement a new habit into our lives. So the best way to apply continued effort over long periods of time is to approach the process in 60-day increments. Put it on your calendar, because reminders work as cues in our lives to push us into action. At the end of each 60-day increment, make time to reassess both small and big goals. Use this time to reassess daily quotas and to choose a new habit that you will begin building into your life using the Implementation Intentions strategy. The process is proven; apply it for maximum results. Whatever you do—choose something. Remaining in constant motion and applying continuous effort is one of Walter's declassified magic keys to success.

As for Walter and his next big-picture goals: he'd tell you, but...

Your life is the sum of your habits. Your happiness is a result of your habits. Your level of success is a result of your habits.

Chapter Twelve

Going the Extra Mile

*Be definite of purpose and go the extra
mile…everything else will fall into place.*

Napoleon Hill has shaped billions of lives. His research brought to light the principles of not just success, but also happiness. Brian Sidorsky highlighted earlier that every time he reads Hill's book *Think and Grow Rich,* he makes another million dollars.

Wow! A book that impactful, that insightful, and that life-changing is rare. Authors with such a profound message are few and far between. Impressed, we wanted to find someone who truly lived the principles behind the bestselling personal development book of all time. But we found something even better—we found the person who has the rights to teach them.

It was 40 years ago when Satish Verma came to North America, having grown up in India. When he was a child, his mother struggled, barely having the money to feed them from one day to the next. While they didn't have much, his mother did have an abundance of one thing—optimism. She shared that optimism with Satish throughout his childhood, constantly reminding him that things would get better.

He chose to believe her, but he knew that in order for things to really get better, he had to have an education. He obtained his degree and a scholarship to a university in Canada. From there, he found success—a sizeable amount of success.

By his own admission, Satish made a lot of money. But due to poor investments, he lost his fortune overnight. Not only did he lose the money he once had, but he owed the bank half a million dollars. It seemed to him to be an impossible situation. He was deep in debt, jobless, and had two children and a wife to support. The only obvious way out seemed to be bankruptcy, which was what he planned to do.

Then he heard about a course that intrigued him. He wanted to attend, but he only had 500 dollars to his name. He had a choice to make—give the 500 dollars to the bank or use 300 dollars to register for the course. His gut feeling told him to take the course.

"During this period in my life, I made a 'foolish' decision to spend the last of my savings on a course based on *Think and Grow Rich*, called 'The Science of Success.' I was laughed at and called a fool for taking this course rather than finding a job, any job, to support my family.

"Only one person trusted me and told me that the decision to take this course would be the best decision I would ever make in my life, saying I would know the value of the knowledge gained from the Science of Success when I became a successful, happy, and prosperous person again. 'You were always a winner and always will be,' he told me, 'and this financial reversal might be the best thing that ever happened to you.' He told me that when I became successful again, I should tell others not to listen to the naysayers who discourage them in difficult times. He also told me to make a promise to him that when this philosophy brought me peace of mind and happiness, I should teach the Science of Success to others so they, too, could learn to throw away the chains of limitations and harness the stupendous power of their own minds to direct to whatever end they choose."

The first lesson Satish learned in the Science of Success changed his life. The subject was definiteness of purpose. He had a purpose—everyone had told him it would take six years after bankruptcy to repair his credit, but Satish wanted to be out of bankruptcy in just six months. And that's precisely what happened. He credits his ability to turn his circumstances around so quickly to the principles he learned in "The Science of Success" from Napoleon Hill's *Think and Grow Rich*.

Moreover, he stood by his promise to teach the Science of Success to others and acquired the rights from the Napoleon Hill Foundation to teach this philosophy to all who are haunted by fear of failure, poverty, and criticism; who lack confidence; and who don't know what power lies dormant within them that needs only a stimulus to be ignited, so they can live a life of purpose and happiness and achieve anything.

Who was this person who believed in Satish when no one else did? We asked him, and he provided us with a telling introduction.

"I want to introduce you to this great person who brought me to where I am today. That person is my inner voice, my spirit, my hopes, my dreams, and my other self. Once you discover your other self, the doors to every possibility become wide open.

When your inner voice tells you to do something, don't wait—just do it, and unlimited opportunities will be waiting for you."

From Satish, we learned that the greatest thing holding us back is ourselves—that inner voice that either supports our goals or holds us back when it is stuck and sometimes sinking. It's the fear of making a wrong decision that gives us the inability to make a decision at all—what we know as paralysis analysis. Sometimes doing the "right" thing isn't the right thing at all. Sometimes we have to venture out of our comfort zone and what is expected of us in order to unlock the opportunities that will lead us to the solution to our problems.

Satish has absolutely no regrets. He not only embraced and applied the principles behind the Science of Success, but he's made them his purpose. He acquired the rights to teach the principles in Canada, hoping that one day he could acquire the rights for the United States, as well. When the opportunity came his way, he didn't hesitate. He followed his own advice and inner voice and jumped on it.

"Like Shakespeare is the master of English literature, our philosophy is the Shakespeare of personal development. The people who have shaped the essence of our world, such as Thomas Edison, Alexander Graham Bell, and Albert Einstein, have shaped this philosophy."

The principles are fascinating, but even more interesting is how they affect the mind. Unless people understand how their mind is impacted, their life will stay the way they have been told their life should be—not the way they want it to be. According to Satish, it is up to you to study and implement the principles behind the Science of Success.

"You can be what you want. You can have anything you want. The only person stopping you is you. You are not taking the steps to make it happen. It takes more than being a seminar junkie—it takes passion and it takes action. The mind is huge—nothing is too big for the mind. The thing that makes a difference is not the mind, but in how big—or little—you think."

Curious, we asked Satish to share what it takes to be, do, or have what one wants. He broke it down into three simple steps:

1. know what you want;

2. have a plan; and

3. if that plan fails, try another plan.

Sounds easy, doesn't it? But we have to agree—we know that simple, persistent pursuit of a goal will create progress. As mentioned earlier in this book, Thomas Edison invented the light bulb. It took him 10,000 failures, but he didn't worry about the failures; he stayed focused on achieving that one success. It took persistence for Edison to create the light bulb, and such a committed will and purpose require a strong desire. It is the magnitude of what we want that makes a difference. The magnitude has to be so huge that failure doesn't stop us from trying. Edison's magnitude was so big that it lit up the entire world.

"Your desire should be a burning desire that transcends everything else in the world. It needs to be a part of you like it's tattooed on your brain. When you're at that level, there is no way you can't succeed," Satish explained. Like Thomas Edison, Satish would not be deterred in his quest to have a mega-successful business. He'd already hit bottom...and he learned a lot because of it. Mostly, he learned that failure is not a permanent status.

"I'm not afraid of failure. I was new to this philosophy when I started teaching the Science of Success, and only one person showed up to my seminar. To me, that wasn't a failure. It was the greatest audience I ever had! My success wasn't defined by the number of seats filled but by the effect I had on the one person in those seats."

What an optimistic attitude! No doubt others in the same situation would have given up and thrown in the towel if that happened to them. But not Satish, who says the secret is all in our mind-set.

"Our problems are so small. People ask how I got out of bankruptcy—what was my driving force? I realized that I was bigger than my problems. If I created a problem, I could solve the problem too. Nothing is bigger than you. You can have, do, or be anything you want. Don't believe in limitations; they don't exist—they exist only in your mind. If fear can exist in your mind, so can success. Replace fear with faith—absolute faith in your ability. Nobody ever really fails. I didn't fail when only one person showed up at my seminar. People only fail when they don't see an equal or better benefit."

Obviously, Satish is the perfect professor to teach Napoleon Hill's success principles. These principles that have been handed to us have been in place forever, though. They have been discovered and rediscovered. Napoleon Hill rediscovered them through the practical example of people who were successful. Satish is now teaching them to a newer generation, making them applicable to and understandable in their world.

What better source to enlighten us about the special secret to success than the person who has the rights to teach the principles identified by the great Napoleon Hill? We know that Hill identified 17 principles of success and achievement, but we were curious to know if one is more powerful than another: If we apply only one of the success principles, which one should we choose?

While a firm believer in implementing all of Hill's principles, Satish was able to identify the two that he believes set the wheels of success in motion: having a definiteness of purpose and going the extra mile.

"Having a definite purpose and going the extra mile encompasses your mental attitude, your pleasing personality, and the faith you have in yourself. Set that goal. Know your purpose. Commit to it. When you set goals in life, there is then only one principle to achieve—go the extra mile. As Napoleon Hill states, your pot of gold is not at the end of the rainbow—it's at the end of the extra mile. If you go the extra mile continuously and don't become complacent, it does something to your conscience and your soul. It's the most powerful principle and exactly how we built our businesses. When you go the extra mile, the other principles fall into place automatically."

A goal is your purpose, whether it is to acquire wealth, open a business, or get out of debt. However, like Hill stated, that purpose must be definite. You must know what it is you want before you can seek and attain it. If you have any doubt, or if your goal or purpose wavers occasionally, so will your commitment and passion. In that case, you will lack the desire and commitment it takes to make it happen.

But once you have that definiteness of purpose, watch out! It becomes your driving force and will influence every decision you make and action you take. Give it your all—*go the extra mile*—and the other success principles will come easily, sometimes with little or no effort on your part.

Why is going the extra mile so important? Going the extra mile means going above and beyond, doing more than is expected. We already know that successful people are willing to do what others aren't, a trait that is common among highly successful entrepreneurs. When you go the extra mile, you are once again exemplifying that you are willing to do what others won't.

Some of the benefits of going the extra mile, according to Napoleon Hill, are:

- It makes one indispensable.

- You see improvement in mental growth and physical skill.

- You have job protection and promotion/raises.

- Through the law of contrast, it makes you more appealing and noticeable than others.

- It develops personal initiative.

However, Hill stated that the greatest benefit of going the extra mile is that it gives the only logical reason to ask for additional compensation. It makes sense that if you do only what you're being paid for and no more, you are worth only what you are getting paid...and no more. We've all heard the age-old excuse of "That's not my job," or "I only get paid to work until

5:00," and when the whistle blows, the biggest rush of energy seen all day is when they're hurrying to leave. These people may have definiteness of purpose, but they aren't willing to go the extra mile and are, therefore, less likely to find their pot of gold.

There are many people who stood out and climbed the ranks based on the principle of going the extra mile. Satish is one. His definiteness of purpose, his goal, was to climb out from under bankruptcy in six short months, instead of the oft experienced six or seven long years. With such a lofty goal, he couldn't waver. Taking his eye off the prize for a single minute would deter him and delay his success. But he did it because he went the extra mile. He not only learned the philosophies of success, but he applied them. He lived them, and he taught them. He worked, and then he worked harder, every minute devoting himself to the fulfillment of his purpose.

Achieving one goal, Satish then set another—to acquire rights to teach Napoleon Hill's Science of Success in Canada, in the United States, and beyond. He has achieved every goal, always ready to do whatever it takes to make it happen. Satish's success can be attributed directly to going the extra mile. He's in good company.

A young man named Frank worked in a dry goods store. During a special sales event, he noticed that some items weren't selling, so he took the personal initiative to gather them and put them on display where everyone could see them. Furthermore, he reduced the price of the items to five or ten cents to encourage their quick sale. It was genius—what couldn't or wouldn't sell behind the counter was now in demand at its lowered price. Customers loved the bargains, but even better, Frank recognized that he was on to something. By doing more than was expected and taking the initiative to test an idea, Frank not only helped his employers move merchandise, but he also recognized that there was a demand for a discount store, what would later be referred to as the "five and dime." Twenty-year-old Frank was on his way to becoming the retail giant and founder of the F.W. Woolworth Company, but he would have never found his pot of gold if he hadn't been willing to go the extra mile.

*Where's your pot of gold? What are you
willing to do to find it?*

Chapter Thirteen

You Can
Change Your World

***You might not be able to change the world,
but surely you can change <u>your</u> world.***

We are each blessed with gifts and a purpose in life. This much we know to be true. What you choose to do with those gifts, whether or not you find your purpose and live it, that is up to you. The majority of people you cross paths with every single day choose a life without purpose. They never lay out goals, and you can't achieve goals that don't exist. These people work jobs they hate, with people they don't care about, for companies they are not emotionally invested in. This lifestyle is very detrimental, so it's easy to understand, knowing this, why so many people end up unhappy.

The cycle of an unhappy existence without purpose or passion is one we hope to help you avoid altogether. Each chapter, thus far, is designed to give you a magic key from someone already living a life of purpose—their very own guiding principle that you can apply to your own life for beneficial results. This chapter is no different. We would like to introduce you to Rita Davenport, a woman from the South with a sense of humor bigger than she is.

When Rita was growing up in Tennessee, she lived in complete poverty. When people would ask her if she knew that she was poor, her answer was always in true Rita form: "Of course I knew," she says. "I was poor, not stupid." The extreme poverty was a cycle her family had been unable to break but one Rita was destined to break. She refers to their poverty as a minor inconvenience, one she overcame to build a life of prosperity, purpose, and a lot of laughter.

When she was just six years old, Rita's aunt made her a dress out of old fifty-pound feed sacks, and the dress quickly became Rita's favorite—so much so that she went around her neighborhood at the time bragging about her new dress and showing it off. The only problem was that Rita was not only blessed with a thick-as-molasses southern drawl, she also had a speech impediment. She tried her hardest to say "feed sack" but it only came out as "theed thack," and her first nickname was born. Now she certainly doesn't have to wear clothes made from sacks anymore, but she has never let this part of herself go, because it's all part of her story and journey to get to where she is now.

Rita has used her early years as motivation and her sense of humor and positive attitude to build a life that is truly remarkable. It seems that everything she touches turns to gold, or maybe that's just the positive spin that she can put on just about anything. Rita credits her sense of humor with being one of the biggest assets in helping her build the life she dreamed of living.

Not only that, but she also uses her sense of humor to reach others and help them attain the life they are seeking.

From 1991 until 2011, Rita was president of Arbonne International and contributed to the growth of sales to over 986 million dollars. Yes, you read that right...almost a billion dollars in sales. Her approach to finding success while working as the president of Arbonne was to make the company a personal development company, a place where everyone involved could go to figure out the best version of themselves and then be that. Her approach was successful, and you cannot walk through the halls of Arbonne today without someone singing her praises for changing the company from the inside out. Even more than that, she changed a lot of lives, and those people who were so lucky to know her say they will never forget her impact on them.

That's not all, either...Rita has achieved some amazing goals in her life. She has shared speakers' platforms with the likes of Dr. John Maxwell, Jack Canfield, Ross Scheffer, Connie Podesta, Erik Weihenmayer, Erma Bombeck, Art Linkletter, Og Mandino, Dr. Joyce Brothers, Tom Hopkins, Zig Ziglar, Les Brown, and Mark Victor Hansen. She has authored several bestselling books, including *Funny Side Up*; *Making Time, Making Money*; *Excellence in Performance*; and *Professionals at Their Best*. She has broadcast two nationally syndicated cable television shows—*Success Strategies* and *Laugh Your Way to Success*—to over 32 million homes across the country...and she's not done yet.

Since Rita retired from Arbonne, she has spent her time traveling the world, using her story to motivate others. She wants everyone to feel good about their gifts and what they bring to the table so they can find their true purpose in life, just as she did.

As Rita puts it, no matter what she is doing, she is always in the "people business." Her passion in life is helping others. "When you put people first, make them feel important, and teach them to believe in themselves, amazing things happen."

Rita is well aware of her gift of reaching others, and she uses it to her full advantage to change the lives of every single person with whom she comes in contact. That's a pretty big order for a woman who grew up in poverty in the South, and she has filled those shoes and then some. What we want to share with you are the secrets to her happiness. We want to break this all down for you and give you the specifics of how you can change *your* world and find great happiness with the tools you already have been blessed with. Rita credits five main practices with helping her build the life she has now, so let's dig in.

1. **Giving:** Rita sums this practice up very nicely: "If you want a rich life, then enrich the lives of others." Giving is reciprocal—like a boomerang, it always comes back to you. By giving, you gain, though that should never be the ultimate goal. Giving should be selfless, an act that is done without an ulterior motive. And it doesn't mean that you need to give money, though money is always welcomed where it is needed. You can give your time, efforts, sponsorship, and support in so many ways. Sure, when you give, the benefactor benefits. The hungry are fed, the homeless are clothed, churches fulfill their missions, the sick and injured receive blood, and people have newfound access to clean water, supplies, and medical care. But consider the flip side—that when you give, you might actually benefit even more than those who receive your gift. Not only does the law of reciprocity return your

abundance to you, sometimes in even greater amounts, but there are mental and physical health benefits, as well.

- People who give to others tend to have lower blood pressure. Studies have shown that those who actively donate their time to causes that are important to them actually live longer than those who don't, with a 44 percent less likelihood of dying within five years.

- Being a giver increases self-esteem while lessening stress and depression.

- Above all, giving activates areas of the brain that are associated with an increase in happiness.

2. **Be on purpose:** Everyone has a purpose and the necessary talents and skills to fulfill it. Finding your major purpose is the key to success and happiness, and it is how you will have a great impact on others. According to Rita, that which you desire you can acquire by defining your purpose and developing your talents to do and achieve more.

3. **Find your sense of humor:** Rita is known for her "Rita-isms," and they are truly hilarious. She had us laughing the entire time we spent with her, and that is one of Rita's ways of making a difference around her. We can never take ourselves too seriously. We have to be able to find humor in life and the situations in which we find ourselves. Laughter is a great tool, and it is also a great way to reach people and change the course of their day.

4. **Impact YOUR world:** We think Rita put it best when she said, "You may not be able to change the world, but you certainly can change your world. So do what you can with what you have to work with. Everyone has talent, and you focus on making an impact in your world with the talent you already have." Sometimes we go too big and we start out with goals of changing the whole world. But change is like the ripple in the pond. The ripples spread far and wide to the very edges of the pond, changing the water we never expected it to change. This is how our impact looks in real life. By affecting people and changing things in your world, you create ripples in the pond, which will most certainly reach further than you ever imagined. Start first by working to change your own world and see where that takes you.

5. **Be grateful:** We hear this all the time from every motivational speaker out there. We see it on T-shirts and coffee mugs. Being grateful is an act that requires effort. A lot of times when people say they are grateful, it is for a brief period of time and it is the result of something having played out in their lives the way they had hoped. This is not what we are talking about. Practicing gratitude full time will change your life in ways you cannot even imagine and in ways we can't even put into words to explain to you. Full-time gratitude takes a little bit of practice to implement. It is a change in your very mind-set by waking up every single day and being grateful for who and where you are in your life before anything goes your way (or doesn't). One of the reasons this is so difficult to maintain is because if there are people around you who don't live like this, they can easily bring you down.

I'm sure you've experienced this several times throughout your life. Just like the energy vampires we talked about in a previous chapter, these people are not willing to put in the effort to live a grateful life and are jealous of and annoyed at those who have chosen the opposite path. They will rain on your parade all day long if you let them, and this can make it difficult to maintain that positive attitude of gratitude. The key to avoiding this is also avoiding people who work to bring you down. You cannot fix them; they don't want to be fixed. You are better off to steer clear and focus on your efforts and attitude.

By applying these practices, you can change your world. When you change your world, you impact the world around you and are better equipped to make a difference everywhere you go. No one was intended to remain the same throughout their entire lives. You were meant to grow and use your talents, skills, and personality to fulfill your mission—your purpose. Injecting your purpose with your unique experiences and personality will put you in a position where you can benefit others. Rita has coupled her humor with the wisdom gained from her life experiences. In doing so, she has turned extreme poverty into a remarkable success, but she never tried to change who she was—that was her secret to success. And she lives it with a healthy dose of laughter.

**Life is a serious business;
living it doesn't have to be.**

Chapter Fourteen

Make a Deal
to Get to the Next Deal

*Climbing the ladder of success,
one rung at a time.*

Many aspiring entrepreneurs put all of their eggs in one basket. They have a single grand idea that they think is going to change their life and make them a fortune. Yes, they're going to be a household name and the next hot thing on the market! And when it happens—and they are sure it will—they'll be set for life and never have to work another day.

If Fred Wagenhals had followed that success formula, true and lasting success would have been elusive. For it wasn't one great idea that changed his life, but several, each progressing him higher up the ladder.

You might not have heard of Fred Wagenhals, but you will recognize the products that he invented and brought to the market, including the jet ski, the four-wheel quad cycle, and NASCAR die-cast miniature cars. It is incredible to be the brains behind such incredible inventions, but it is even more amazing when one looks at Fred's past.

According to his high school principal, Fred would never amount to anything. A poor student, he ranked near the bottom of his class. His college career was short; he quit after just one quarter, leaving before they had a chance to kick him out. One of the compelling reasons behind that decision came from one of his professors. When Fred asked how much money she made, she answered $18,000. "How are you going to teach me to be a millionaire then?" he asked.

Fred did receive an education, but it wasn't from books or postsecondary institutions. He found a mentor to take him under his wing—a man who pulled up into his family's driveway in a convertible, accompanied by a pretty blonde. The man was a tool and die salesman who was paying a visit to Fred's father, who had a tool and die job for Whirlpool. Instantly, Fred knew that he wanted to be a tool and die salesman, and he begged the man to teach him everything he knew.

For the next four years, that's exactly what happened. Fred accompanied the salesman, who taught him some very important lessons, which unbeknownst to him would have a tremendous impact on his later success. The first lesson was: Take a job and finish it. Even if you lose money on that job, finish what you started.

Fred's entrepreneurial career then progressed, and he opened a tool and die design business. From there, he delved into snowmobile design—a business that brought him his first success when he designed and patented a jet pump boat. But Fred ran out of money. Needing to pay his employees, he sold the patent for $75,000. Eventually, his invention became the now-famous Bombardier Jet Ski.

Most people would think that Fred would regret selling his invention for such a low price. After all, the personal watercraft industry is worth billions. It's easy for us to think that he should be kicking himself—after all, he could have hit the Holy Grail and been set for life!

Fred's thought process was unconventional, but quite possibly the key to his ultimate success. He needed money to pay his employees (who, by the way, he claims are his biggest assets). In addition, he needed money to get to the next deal. Far from kicking himself, Fred is confident that it was the right decision at the time. It was necessary if he was going to get to the next deal. Fred didn't follow the conventional thinking that he had only one shot at success. No, he was always pursuing something bigger, something better.

And he found it...one step at a time. The $75,000 he got from selling his jet ski patent allowed him to design the four-wheel quad cycle, which he sold to Jeep Corporation, who later sold it to Honda. Again, he didn't make a fortune, but he did make enough to stay in business.

It was a chance meeting with a champion bull rider that came next. The bull rider invited Fred to go to Hollywood with him, where he would be teaching an actor how to ride a mechanical bull for a movie. The actor was John Travolta, who starred in the hit movie *Urban Cowboy*. Once Fred saw the bull, he knew he could design something much better. Returning home, that's exactly what he did. Fred bought 200 sets of parts and sold the mechanical bulls across the country. He'd then buy them back at a fraction of the price and resell them overseas, creating additional revenue from a single product.

Fred's adventures also introduced other inventions, such as the car he designed for actor Hervé Villechaize, whose character, Tattoo, drove it on television's *Fantasy Island.*

One would think those accomplishments are plenty, and rightfully so—to most of us, Fred has enjoyed significant success. Yet individually, they were base hits, not grand slams, and Fred knew that. Thankfully, he is a forward thinker. He's always thinking of the next deal and looks upon each success as a necessary step that will lead him to it.

He was on an airplane when the next big idea came to him. After reading an article about baseball trading cards being a half-a-billion-dollar-a-year market, he wondered why someone hadn't painted a little diecast car to mimic those of famous race car drivers and paired each with a trading card. Neither diecast cars nor trading cards were new; both had been around for decades. But nobody had paired them together to represent a growing sport—NASCAR racing. Fred was onto something. His previous inventions and designs had introduced him to many people, including championship NASCAR driver Dale Earnhardt. Fred asked him for an exclusive license in exchange for $300,000. Earnhardt agreed to the deal...but there was just one problem. Fred didn't have the money.

True to his beliefs, Fred understood that you've got to make a deal to get to a better deal. So he sold his house to pay Earnhardt for the exclusive license. Was it worth it? In eight short years, Fred Wagenhals took his diecast racing cars to $407 million a year in sales. In 2005, he sold the company for $245 million.

Now, that's the financial Holy Grail. It's a grand slam, out-of-the-park home run—the kind where you can kick your feet up and take a year, a decade, or the rest of your life off, if you want. The problem is Fred doesn't want to stop working. Getting up and going to work every day is a ritual for him. He might have hit the ball in the sweet spot, but to Fred, it was simply a way to get to the next deal. And every day, he is hot on the pursuit of the next big deal and excited to find out where that will lead him.

How does Fred do it? How does he manage to climb the ladder of success continually, each time reaching higher levels than the last? We asked him, and he shared the keys that have brought him such great success:

1. **Hire key people.** Fred is well aware that his employees are assets that hold more value than money. Many of his deals centered around being able to pay them and keep them on his staff. "I was fortunate enough to be at the top of the action. I was smart enough to hire the people who made it happen," he states.

2. **Never quit.** "If you threw me out into a desert with nothing, I'd find my way back," he said. Fred knows what many entrepreneurs don't recognize: success is not a one-shot opportunity. There is always another chance. Even after enjoying his successes, Fred is still at it. Like he says, "The dream might change, but there's always a dream." He gets up every morning and is at his desk by 6:00 a.m. It's a part of the ritual that keeps him focused and accomplished.

3. **Never let anyone outwork you.** Work as hard as you have to and then some. Lead by example, and others will follow

suit. For Fred, the work must go on—he makes a list of things to do every day and he checks them off, one by one. In doing so, he is able to see the progress that's being made, one step at a time.

When you follow Fred's theory, every success, no matter how large or how small, is a step toward something bigger. Becoming an overnight success on your very first try is the exception, not the rule. Start by getting your feet wet, then let each success propel you to the next. You just have to recognize the fact that not every deal is going to be a home run, but base hits will get you to home plate, too.

Sometimes, success comes in steps. Unfortunately, most people want to be an overnight success. They want to wake up one day with the realization that they've suddenly "made it." But very few of us are discovered suddenly and catapulted like a rocket ship to fame. And when it doesn't happen like we dreamed it would, discouragement sets in. We doubt ourselves and take our eyes off our goal, not realizing that we were on track to reach it... we just needed to persevere and have faith in the process.

We're all a work in progress. At the age of 15, Leonardo da Vinci began developing his painting career. He spent ten years as an apprentice, learning and perfecting his craft before he painted his first commissioned piece of art. His most famous paintings, *The Last Supper* and the *Mona Lisa*, weren't painted until he was well into his forties and fifties. It took more than four decades for da Vinci to be ready to create the world's most famous and admired paintings. Imagine what would have happened if da Vinci had given up when his first, second, or fortieth painting didn't become an overnight masterpiece. Imagine how much different Fred's life would have been if he hadn't sold his jet ski patent for $75,000, viewing that deal as an asset that was necessary for future ideas. He's a prime example of the theory that no success is too small. When a deal is good for both parties, it's the secret that will get you there—one deal at a time.

> **Success is a journey…always be thinking of the next deal and look upon each success as a necessary step that will lead you to it.**

Chapter Fifteen

Permission to Live Your Passion

Be a part of something bigger than yourself.

Continuing our quest to find the magic key to living a life of sustained abundance, one story deeply touched our hearts. So often we encounter people who want to be successful in order to improve their lot in life. On occasion, though, we are privileged to know someone whose success is entirely driven by the desire to help others. Douglas Jackson is the perfect example. Douglas, however, was not immune from the desire to be personally wealthy. He has tasted that success from both sides, as his quest for personal wealth was replaced with the riches that come from making a difference in the lives of others.

Douglas's story starts with his parents. It is unique, fascinating, and begs to be told.

His father grew up in Iowa in a family that was very poor—so poor that he set a goal that consumed him: to be a millionaire by the time he was 30 years old. Unfortunately, he missed his goal and didn't become a millionaire until he was 31. Douglas recalls those years, stating that nearly everything his parents did was centered around the pursuit of accumulating money and achieving their millionaire status.

His parents achieved their goal by being entrepreneurs. Douglas was only in the fourth grade when he set his own goal: he wanted to be a lawyer. He completed college in two years and went on to complete law school two years later. He set out to build his career as an attorney, but then he discovered something—people were making more money than he was! Not to be outdone, he went back to college to follow suit in his new goal to be a rich investment banker.

During Douglas's quest to achieve his goals, his millionaire parents made a shocking discovery: they were rich, but they weren't happy. In a surprise move, they followed their hearts and created a foundation. One Saturday morning, they sat Douglas and his brother at the kitchen table and told them they'd given all of their money away. The all-important dollar suddenly held little, if any, value to them. As a result, their sons had no inheritance.

People so often chase the almighty dollar in their quest for happiness. Refusing to believe that money doesn't buy happiness, they are steadfast in their pursuit to dispel the myth. Surely, they will be the one to prove it wrong, and when they claim their financial fortune, their woes will be a thing of the past. Money will provide for their every need and pave their way to a life of contentment and happiness.

Until they learn differently…

Douglas's father found that money is a necessity, but having it is not what creates happiness. For him, money without a purpose was a burden, not a dream. This knowledge is what eventually created his happiness and fueled his desire to be a part of something bigger than himself.

Douglas's father set out to find his purpose. Before long, he was using his financial knowledge to benefit others as an economic consultant who traveled across the world. He visited a clinic in an impoverished foreign country, and Douglas's father was shocked to find it empty. There was no equipment, no supplies, and no medicine. With a promise to help, his dad returned to the States and kept his word. His garage became a warehouse for donations and supplies, but he wanted to do more, and in an attempt to make a greater contribution, he asked Douglas for help. Admiring his father's passion in the pursuit of selflessly helping others, Douglas agreed to devote six months to the cause; then, he could return to his career and devote his time to the pursuit of his personal wealth.

They applied for and received a $75,000 grant, and Douglas got a few others to help them. That was 18 years ago. Their foundation, Project Cure, started in his parents' garage and now sends a semi-truck trailer of medical supplies every other day to 133 countries. They have attracted thousands of volunteers yet have only 25 staff members. A remarkable feat, their foundation has been named by *Forbes* as one of the top 200 charities in America.

Douglas walked away from his career and has never looked back. When asked what drives him, he stated that he sees people who are hurting, and it's a story that deserves to be told. They have an opportunity to change the course of history by saving lives. Through their foundation, they have helped to reduce maternal mortality in Third World countries by 61 percent and given new life to cancer patients who would otherwise die within one year of diagnosis. With each person they help, they recognize a need to do more and are invigorated with a renewed sense of energy. The need has touched the lives of their volunteers, who now number 17,000, which inspired the question, "How do you get so many people to devote their time and efforts to your cause, especially when they're not being paid?" His answer brings us to Douglas's magic key—the reason why he continues to do what he does every single day.

People work for passion or purpose.

We're all inspired by money, but like a good pizza, the first slice is the best. After that, it has less impact. At some point, the next dollar has less impact than the previous one. This is especially true if you don't have a purpose. If you have no reason for doing what you do, you will never be happy. Douglas has gone from CEO to chief storytelling officer to help refuel their volunteers' purpose by bringing in people from the countries they serve who attest to the fact that they are directly benefitting others. Those stories are what drives him every day.

The magic key for people like Douglas and his father is finding their purpose and passion. They wanted to create a legacy that was bigger than life and change the course of history. Perhaps that is the greatest gift they can bestow on mankind. As Douglas aptly states, "Who knows, the people whose lives we change might be future Nobel Peace Prize winners. By saving a mother, we can change an entire family's course of history."

It's only natural to doubt that we can have that much impact on mankind. After all, there is power in numbers. But when our passion is strong and our purpose is genuine, we can do small things in a very big way. Douglas admits that it was audacious for them to take a risk and pursue such a lofty dream. He also admits that they made mistakes along the way, but they kept at it, and much like Thomas Edison in his relentless pursuit to invent the light bulb, they never quit.

For people like Douglas, wealth is not about money. True wealth lies in the thing that makes one really happy. It's the thing that wakes you up and makes you feel blessed. Abundance does not lie in the size of your bank account or paycheck, but in the opportunity to share it. Douglas shares how to create your abundance:

1. DO WHAT COMES EASY FOR YOU.

"People will do more for a cause they are passionate about than they will do for money," states Douglas. "To find the magic key to your abundance, find the thing that seems easy to you. That's your sweet spot. Nobody had to convince Michael Jordan to play basketball, and he made it look so easy. Stop focusing on strengthening your weaknesses and focus instead on the thing that you love and that comes easy for you. That's what you'll do best."

2. GIVE YOURSELF PERMISSION TO LIVE YOUR PASSION.

Too often, we try to live up or down to others' expectations. A parent might want us to go to college and be a doctor, a lawyer, or a CPA, and we feel pressured to follow their wishes. If it's not what you want to do, you won't be happy...and you probably won't be good at it. Do what you love, and you will be good at it.

3. IF IT SCARES YOU, DO IT ANYWAY.

Don't let fear stand in your way. Fear is nothing more than an emotion, albeit a powerful emotion that is capable of thwarting any dream. Fear tricks you into thinking you're simply delaying your success and abundance, but in actuality it will put the brakes on them and bring you to a total halt. Even if you hold the magic key to your dreams, you cannot open them if you're too scared of what's on the other side. If you're scared, do it anyway. Powerful emotions are indicators of life-changing pursuits. View fear as a sign that something phenomenal is about to happen. The greater the emotion, the greater the reward.

4. ASK YOURSELF IF YOU WOULD RATHER DO SOMETHING ELSE.

If your answer is "yes," then don't waste another minute before you chase that dream. Life is too short to waste on something that doesn't fulfill your purpose and passion. If your answer is "no," then keep doing what you're doing. Give it 100 percent and more, for this is precisely what you were put here for and part of the legacy you are intended to leave behind.

Your purpose and passion are unique to you—they will dictate your legacy. It is your job to find out what they are. Once you do, you'll hold the magic key to your abundance. It may take time to be led to your purpose, but you will find it. If you don't, it will find you. Douglas's purpose found him. Even when he was busy chasing another dream, he kept going back to his passion and purpose until he realized that was where he belonged and gave himself permission to live his passion. With that blessing, he unlocked the door to an abundance far greater than financial wealth. It was there that he found the key to happiness.

> ***Are you waiting to find your passion, or
> is it already there, waiting for you to give
> yourself permission to live it to its fullest?***

Chapter Sixteen

Unstoppable

Becoming unstoppable by
generating the law of giving.

Our journey to find the magic key that creates and sustains abundance has introduced us to some incredible people with fascinating stories. When most of us think of success on such a scale, we think of people who have built their fortunes through entrepreneurship, people who have created businesses or products that have achieved great success and made them what they are today. But our search has told us something different, too. Sure, there are plenty of people who turned ideas into dollars and created phenomenal businesses with those ideas. Yet there are others—people like Douglas Jackson—who chose a nonconventional route. Instead of selling products and services, they have mastered the entrepreneurship of movements and missions that help others. For some, the goal isn't about creating personal success but instead about being successful in their desire to help others.

Napoleon Hill once said, "It is literally true that you can succeed best and quickest by helping others to succeed." Hill wasn't speaking only of philanthropy through the contributions of money, but also in giving of our time, effort, and knowledge. Knowledge is the greatest asset we own. When knowledge and experience combine for the sole purpose of empowering others, its value is beyond comparison. Those who grasp this concept and implement it in their lives understand that this is the magic key that unlocks infinite abundance.

Cynthia Kersey has built a foundation around this principle. As the founder of the Unstoppable Foundation, she has been instrumental in improving lives and giving people the knowledge and tools they need in all areas of their lives. One inspiration led to her profound calling and breakthrough.

Cynthia quit her job in corporate America, cashed in her entire life savings, and downsized her life to write her first book, *Unstoppable.* She had a very successful career and enjoyed being at the top of her field at Sprint Communications, where she had reached the high position of national account manager. Yet she wasn't happy about or inspired by her life. She was inspired by people who were unstoppable. And she wanted to write a book and tell the world their stories.

Although Cynthia had never written anything more challenging than a college term paper, she wrote her book—a goal many don't ever accomplish. Two and a half years later, her book was published, another commendable feat, especially for a first-time author. She admits that she experienced rejection and discouragement but states it was the inspiration of the unstoppable people she interviewed for her book that kept her going. If they were unstoppable, she could be, too. Her stickability landed her a publisher, and Cynthia's dream came true. She was free to live her purpose and enjoy the fruits of her success.

For a short while, at least. A year and a half after her book was released, her marriage of 20 years ended. Devastated, she called her mentor, who told her, "When you have a great pain in your life, you need a greater purpose." He then offered an unusual suggestion: Why don't you build a house for a family in need?

Her mentor had just returned from Nepal, which he described as one of the most beautiful, and impoverished, countries in the world. Thinking about what he'd said, Cynthia considered building a house for a family in Nepal, but the thought wasn't enough to lessen her pain. So she wondered how many houses she would have to build to offset the pain she was experiencing. It wasn't until she got to 100 that she felt the number was bigger than her pain.

There was just one thing standing in her way. Cynthia was a single mother who was living on the revenues from a $14.95 book. A new author, she didn't have a monumental mailing list or a network of people with an abundance of money to share. She had no understanding of how it would be possible for her to fund a project of such a grand scale. The concept of building 100 houses was far outside her paradigm. She didn't have a clue as to how she was going to make it happen, but she did have a vision and was committed to it.

Her purpose was bigger than her pain, and that propelled her forward. So Cynthia called another friend and mentor, Bob Proctor, who told her the solution was easy. Each house would cost $2,000—all she had to do was find 10 people to donate $20,000 each toward her mission. With all of the courage she could muster, she found the nerve right then and there to start soliciting donations, asking Bob if he would be the first to donate $20,000. With a gulp, he agreed to the unanticipated request. Not only did she have the solution, but she had already met 10 percent of her goal!

While she was healing and speaking about being unstoppable, she continued to share her purpose and find donors for her project. After raising the necessary $200,000, she took 18 people to Nepal and built the first three of the 100 homes that they would build that year. That experience fundamentally changed her life because she thought she was doing something great for the Nepalese people, but she hadn't anticipated how much it would change her life.

It was also when she started learning about the law of giving and receiving.

"The scriptures say, 'Give and it shall be given unto you.' We live in a world of scarcity, though, so people think they can't give now—they will wait until they have money, until their kids get out of school, or until their business picks up. What really happens, though, is receiving is activated by giving. It's not the reverse. If you're waiting and holding on and don't feel like you have the money, you're in the energy of contraction."

Cynthia is proof that the law of giving and receiving works. Even though her intention was to complete the project, not to make money, she made more money that year than she had in her last year at Sprint Communications, where she had earned a six-figure income.

This sparked Cynthia's curiosity into the law of giving and receiving and the law of contribution. Studying and seeing models of people who were guided by these laws changed her life even more.

In 2005, when her next book, *Unstoppable Women,* was released, she started looking for another philanthropic project. In the meantime, she was invited to attend a conference in Kenya. The only thing she knew about the conference was that women from East Africa were meeting with women from North America to share their stories. She had no idea what to expect, but something told her she had to be there.

Cynthia spent five days in rural Kenya, where she heard stories that broke her heart and changed her life—tragic stories about poverty, hardships, and the lack of health care. She cried with mothers who had lost their children to malaria because they had no health care facilities. She was appalled that children had to drink contaminated water or spend their entire day fetching and hauling water. The one constant that she heard among these women is that their biggest obstacle was a lack of education. The No. 1 hope among the African women was getting their kids an education, because without it, nothing changes.

These stories opened Cynthia's eyes, and she wondered how it was fair that one's birthplace would determine the quality of their life and their access to the most basic needs. The unfairness stayed with her until the conference was over, but it seemed to her that she would never have the ability to make an impact on the problems that plagued these women. However, when parting ways, the women hugged and the African women asked one thing of her—"please don't forget us"—and Cynthia vowed that she would not.

Back home, she tried to figure out what she could do—after all, the problems were too many, too large, and she was just one person. Then she received inspiration from a friend, whose son requested that people give to a specific cause rather than giving him gifts for his Bar Mitzvah. She had her solution!

Her 50th birthday was approaching, so she threw herself a birthday party, requesting donations rather than gifts. People made a donation to get in the door, and the donations generously continued throughout the night. In one night, she raised $80,000. It was enough to fund two schools. People were actually thanking her for the opportunity to give and make a lasting contribution to the lives of children across the world.

But Cynthia wasn't done. If she could raise $80,000 in one night, what could she do if she really put her mind to it? After doing some research, she learned that in a developing country, schools were typically empty in three to five years, and for good reason—those kids didn't have access to clean water. They were home fetching water or were sick from drinking contaminated water. They weren't getting fed and were hungry and malnourished. They had no access to health care and were sick and unable to learn.

She also discovered another obstacle—if the parents didn't know how to generate an income, the project could not be sustainable. Instead of just building a school, she knew she had to focus on all five pillars. In order to deliver on her promise to the African women, Cynthia had to expand her purpose.

After partnering with another organization that provided those five pillars, Cynthia's foundation has educated more than 50,000 people, which includes more than 33,000 children. They help fund two high schools and are funding the first college in the entire area to help the citizens gain the knowledge and skills to generate an income and become leaders.

By being inspired by unstoppable people, Cynthia has become unstoppable. No longer adding books to her *Unstoppable* series, she now focuses entirely on the Unstoppable Foundation. She says it would not have happened if she hadn't listened to that still, small voice within and had the courage to pursue her dreams.

"When you have the calling and the capacity to make it a reality, you have to have the courage to say 'yes,'" she states. "First, look for opportunities to give. I'm very inspired by giving. It's the greatest thing you can do. If you're going to do something like this, you really have to be inspired by it. You have to be willing to listen, because inspiration and opportunities come all of the time. You have to be aware. Mary Morrissey talks about noticing what you're noticing. I chose to notice the possibility, instead of being a victim. That conversation inspired me."

What inspires you? What makes you happy? To learn the answer, Cynthia recommends an exercise in self-discovery from her book. Ask yourself the following questions to give yourself clarity:

- What do you want to be a part of, and what do you want your life to be about?

- What is the group of people you most want to serve? Is it children, women, minorities, or those who are ill or disadvantaged?

- What is the verb that most inspires you—in other words, what is the action you most want to take? It could be writing, building, organizing, or listening. This will lead you toward what you want to *do.*

- What is the end result you desire?

Cynthia found clarity through inspiration. Her experiences reveal that inspiration and the law of giving are not two independent entities—they actually go together. "I've received so much and am so blessed from giving. It's a perpetual cycle. When you come from that place where you aren't giving from obligation, but from inspiration, it's a divine calling, a divine inspiration, that becomes generative, not depleting."

After writing two books about unstoppable people, Cynthia knows what it takes to be unstoppable. "People have a misperception that to be unstoppable, you have to have superpowers or have amazing skills, but what I found to be true is that when you have a purpose—something that is bigger than you—and you commit to it, you will be successful." Cynthia had no idea how to write a book, raise money, or start a foundation. She had no reason to believe she would be successful. But she was committed. Once one is committed, it's like divine providence moves in, and things start happening to support you that you couldn't have imagined. But those things won't come until you make a decision and are committed.

"When you're saying 'yes' to things you're guided by, no matter how small they are, and you make a commitment, things come forward. You'll find the answers, but you won't find them in the resources until after you make the commitment. Some people believe they have to be shown the way before they will make a commitment, but it's the other way around."

You have to believe in the unseen. That's when your life and successes unfold. That's when your magic key opens doors and your vision gains momentum.

When knowledge and experience combine for the sole purpose of empowering others, the value is beyond comparison. That's when you become unstoppable.

Chapter Seventeen

Set Milestones

***Life is not filled with finish lines;
it is filled with milestones.***

This is your life. What is your legacy worth to you? Is it worth the sacrifice, the time, and the mental and physical effort required to create it? Are you willing to do whatever it takes to make it happen...or will you allow a wall of fears to create an impenetrable barrier that stands between you and your goals?

In this book, we've met some incredible people with seemingly impossible accomplishments. One thing they all had in common was a desire that was stronger than their fears. They will all tell you that success is not easy—the amount of inspiration, perspiration, and endurance required will make most give up before they can claim victory. However, none of those requirements ultimately stood between them and their accomplishments. Neither did the greatest impediment to success—that impediment is none other than fear.

No one knows more about fears than James Lawrence. His journey began as a triathlon racer, or more specifically, as an Ironman racer. The Ironman is a grueling triathlon, deemed to be the most difficult sporting event in the world. It consists of a 2.4-mile swim, followed by a 112-mile bicycle ride, and then a full 26.2-mile marathon—all without taking a break. In addition, it must be completed within 17 hours. Few attempt it; fewer accomplish it. One man, however, is an even rarer exception. That man is James Lawrence. In his journey, he encountered fear all of the time—fear that knocked him down and threatened his survival nearly every day.

Being an Ironman is about more than racing and endurance—for James, it is part of his core beliefs. His story is not about his accomplishment; it's about the little things he does and the people he impacts on his journey. For his goal became much larger than a sporting event—it was inspiring others to make the impossible possible and to create milestones so high they are bigger than life and larger than their fears.

James describes an Ironman event as physically and mentally intense. It requires hard work, sacrifice, pain, and endless hours of training. To him, it is worth it because the feeling upon each completion of the 140-mile test of extreme physical endurance is so exhilarating that he wanted to have that feeling as often as he could. More than that, he wanted to create a legacy, so he set out to break the world record for the most Ironman Triathlons completed in one year.

In race six, he thought he'd met his match. Coming out of the water in 12th place, he jumped on his bike and overtook the leaders. He was doing well until he hit the 100th mile and his right leg cramped. Quitting was not an option, so he pedaled the remaining bicycle portion with his left leg. Then, he went on to the marathon. Only 26.2 miles to go and this Ironman would be a wrap. The more he ran, though, the more he knew something was wrong. His body wasn't reacting the way it should, and it completely broke down at mile 17, when every muscle in his body contracted, causing him to hit the ground and lose consciousness. While medical personnel tended to him, a friend handed him a phone so he could speak to his nine-year-old daughter, Lucy.

"Dad, can you walk?" she asked. He replied that he could not.

"Dad, can you crawl?" she continued. Again, the answer was no.

"Dad, can you cartwheel?"

Something hit him and he realized at that moment that if a nine-year-old child had so much belief and conviction that she actually believed he could cartwheel for nine miles, he could find a way to complete the race. He got up and began walking, and when he got about 100 feet away, he paid tribute to his daughter and cartwheeled to the finish line.

With his resolve and the belief others had in him, he completed 30 Ironman races that year, breaking the previous world record of 20. Yet that wasn't enough—James realized that he hadn't pushed himself to his own satisfaction. He hadn't found his physical or mental limits. That's when he came up with the idea of 50–50–50: 50 Ironman Triathlons in 50 days in 50 states.

He told everyone he knew, and every single person said it was impossible. It simply could not be done. They said he'd physically hurt himself; doctors claimed he would die. If he defied the odds and held up physically, he would succumb to mental exhaustion. Then, they pointed out that logistics would shut him down: there was no way he could travel to a new state every day, for 50 days in a row, without mechanical or other difficulties.

James points out that his mind-set had to be infallible. Failure was not an option. In order to succeed, he had to follow his plan. He advises that achieving any goal requires the need to be creative, intelligent, and able to pivot. Like so many had forewarned when he announced his goal, obstacles will come. In order to overcome them, you have to set a goal so big that you go in swinging and don't stop—even if it's something you've never done before.

When was the last time you did something for the first time? Do you remember when you last stepped outside of your comfort zone? Are you afraid to move across the country, change careers, or launch a business? Moving out of our comfort zone is frightening. The struggle, as they say, is real. James admits that it is scary. Everyone has a "hard," and everyone's "hard" is different. Your hard is very real, but you can overcome it if you face that fear.

Compared to what James experienced, our goals and fears might seem trivial. Regardless, they are real. Like James, we have the power to take action to dispel our fears and move closer to our dream.

One reason many of us don't achieve our goals is because they're not big enough to light a fire that won't wane. When we set out to achieve something, we have to want it badly enough that nothing will stand in our way. That is true whether the goal is to lose 20 pounds or climb Mt. Kilimanjaro. If we don't want it bad enough, we won't take the steps necessary to make it happen. This is especially true when obstacles threaten.

John D. Rockefeller wasn't a stranger to obstacles. His father left his family for days, even weeks at a time to spend time with his "other" family. Often left to fend for himself, young John got his first job as an assistant bookkeeper at the age of 16. He meticulously wrote down every dollar he earned and kept track of his savings, expenses, and investments. Then the Panic of 1857 hit and wiped it all out.

That's an obstacle beyond anyone's control. It's one that would stop most of us in our tracks. For nearly everyone, it created massive fear—everyone, that is, except for John D. Rockefeller, who was grateful that it happened. "Oh, how blessed young men are who have to struggle for a foundation and beginning in life. I shall never cease to be grateful for the three and a half years of apprenticeship and the difficulties to be overcome, all along the way."

Rockefeller used the panic as an opportunity to become educated about finances and investments. He realized that most people are easily swayed by public perception and opinion. This insight actually led him to thrive during economic disasters, and within 20 years, 90 percent of the oil market was in his control. When asked, he credited his success to one thing—being able to see opportunity in every disaster.

Obstacles are real, but they can be overcome one step at a time. Accomplishments that leave a legacy aren't realized in their completion—they are only achievable one increment at a time. As James stated, it took many steps to set his record.

Life is not filled with finish lines; it is filled with milestones.

James had many milestones, but none could have been accomplished without an incredibly supportive crew who kept him on track. From his daughter, who ran alongside him, to the people who drove him from state to state and tended to his medical, physical, and mental needs, there was someone with him at all times to help him through the next hurdle.

There will always be obstacles. Like James said, the goal was always to complete 50 Ironman Triathlons in 50 days in 50 states, but there were a thousand opportunities to reduce that to 48 or less. More than a few times, he fell asleep on his bike and dropped to the ground; the police pulled him over and told him that he couldn't keep going. On day one, he could have given up when he became violently ill for two days. Down the stretch, exhaustion and 106 degree heat knocked him down. At times, he was terrified. He had to decide if he was going to face his fears and keep going or pack it up and go home. He kept going—his legacy was worth it.

Achieve greatness by setting a goal so big that it scares you, and be so naïve that you don't have a clue how to make it happen. But always be unstoppable. Keep going. When your dream is that big, there is no other option.

Did James put himself through mental and physical torture and exhaustion just to prove he could? No. He did it because he wanted to help build others up and show them that they, too, can accomplish their goals and achieve their dreams, no matter how lofty they are or how many people say it cannot be done. He wanted his story to resonate with a few people, hoping the ripple effect would make it resonate with others. He knew that the influence could be great, and it drove him to continue, despite his pain and fear.

James is a testament to the fact that fear paralyzes. On day 20, it caused him to lay on the ground and weep—he hurt that badly. But he knew one thing that most people don't: Everything you want is on the other side of fear. A better you is on the other side of fear.

Your legacy is on the other side of your fears. When you want something so much that it is bigger than your fear, you'll find a way to do the seemingly impossible. When others say it can't be done, your legacy will prove otherwise.

It's your life. Before you cross the finish line, push through your fears and create your legacy, one milestone at a time.

Magic is waiting…in the milestones.

Chapter Eighteen

Change the World

How one man, with one simple act of kindness, changed the world.

You can change the world. We have shared the magic keys to success from many different perspectives. Each story reveals opportunities for us to learn and expand our vision so that we can better recognize opportunities that come our way. But this story shares how a simple act of kindness created the magic key to changing the lives of millions of children.

In 1980, there was a young boy by the name of Chris who was living out his final days after being diagnosed with childhood leukemia. Chris had one dying wish—to be a highway patrol motorcycle officer, and with the help of the local community and the Arizona Highway Patrol his wish came true. What happened that day, and in the days to follow, was truly magical and is difficult to put into words.

Part of the team helping to make this young boy's wish come true was Frank Shankwitz. Frank realized something tremendous

---

when he helped to fulfill that first wish—he could change the world through simple acts of kindness. With that realization, Frank decided he wanted to start a nonprofit foundation that would let children diagnosed with critical illnesses "make a wish" and have it come true. The Make-A-Wish Foundation came to life, and today it is one of the largest and most well-known children's charities in the world.

What we've learned from Frank is that perhaps there is no major task staring us down each day as we try to tackle our life's purpose. What if it was simpler than that? What if small acts of kindness were the actual key to our impact on the world? With what started as one small wish, Frank found a way to help children realize their dreams before it was too late.

In 1980, there is no way Frank could have known how his role, in that one event, could cause ripples so large that they would be felt and talked about around the world. When Frank participated in fulfilling that first wish, he forever changed that child's life and his own. With wishes, he and his foundation have put magic and hope in the lives of children who, in their darkest moments, are in dire need of that light and love.

Through the Make-A-Wish Foundation, Frank has had the opportunity to create ripples so great that there will never be a way to fully comprehend just how many lives he has touched. Life has a funny way of letting us forget how important it is to use each day to enrich the world around us. It isn't easy to focus on leading a meaningful and passionate life, but it is necessary if your wish is to make an impact and leave a legacy.

Our purpose is our impact. We have all been tasked with leaving the world better than we found it, and we do this through the ripples *we* make and the lives we change. Every single day is an opportunity to change a life. Let Frank show you how your life can be a gift to the world around you through simple acts of kindness. You will feel your heart and soul come to life as you realize the impact *you* can make.

Remember…one small wish started it all.

Chapter Nineteen

Determination to Win

You have, in your own power, in your mind, the capacity to acquire whatever you want.

The entrepreneurs, business owners, and success experts we met and interviewed have shared their magic keys to success. As you probably noted, there isn't just one magic key to success. In fact, many keys will unlock that door—it is up to you to find the one that works best for you.

While we were overwhelmed by the incredible success stories we heard and the phenomenal advice we gained in our quest to find the "magic key" to success, we also knew that no single personal or professional book on the topic would be complete without including its founding father, Napoleon Hill, who shared his achievement principles in what is still the bible of success, *Think and Grow Rich*. While most of us have read and studied those principles time and time again, we wanted to find Hill's one magic key—the one key to success that rose above all others. We started this book with the magic key of concentration, but our quest uncovered a lecture in which the great Napoleon Hill shared another magic key that, when combined with concentration, will unlock any door to success. Rather than telling you what it is, we've included below the transcript of that lecture, given to insurance salesmen employed by Hill's partner, W. Clement Stone, so that you can learn it from the master.

More than forty years ago, I started out with the richest and the most successful man in the world to give the world a new philosophy of individual achievement based upon the knowhow gained by men through a lifetime of experience by the trial and error method. That philosophy, when it was completed, now under the title of Science of Success, consisted of 17 principles. Now those principles were not ideas of mine, not something that I concocted or invented. They were principles that were discovered by men like Henry Ford and Thomas A. Edison and Andrew Carnegie and Henry J. Kaiser and W. Clement Stone and other outstanding men who have made great successes in the world. If I undertook to talk to you about 17 principles, you probably wouldn't remember any of them. It would be quite unusual if you did. I'm not going to talk to you about 17 principles. I'm going to talk to you about one principle wherein you can resolve all 17 of those principles. And the purpose of those 17 is to help you develop this one thing that I'm going to talk to you about. That's the thing without which you will never succeed no matter how much training you get here, and incidentally, you're getting plenty, and it's very wonderful. But you'll never be a success unless you acquire this one trait that I'm going to talk to you about.

I've seen Mr. Stone perform miracles in the last five years that I've been associated with him. I've seen young fellows come in here who never made over $75 or $100 a week, and I've seen him step them up to where they can make $1,000 a week; yes, even $1,300 a week, as much as the president of the United States makes. I've seen that happen. I think I know how it happened. It happened because he enabled those individuals to develop this trait that I'm going to talk to you about. And before I tell you what that trait is, I wish you would put down in your notes the one thing you think you need above everything else in order to succeed in this particular work you're going into—the one outstanding thing, not two things. I don't want two or three; I only want one. The one thing, the one quality, the one thing that you will need above everything else, and incidentally the thing that I'm going to give you, is something that you can have just for the asking. It's not something you have to acquire through painstaking labor over a long period of years. You can have it instantaneously by willing to have it. That gives you a pretty good clue as to what it is, too, doesn't it? Almost spelled it out.

I have made it my business down through the years to write mottos, epigrams, and state a great truth in as few words as possible, and I think perhaps the most outstanding one that I ever wrote is the one that you have seen around here, and if you haven't, you will see it in the literature that goes out. Now that, to a lot of people, might seem like just a frivolous assembly of words. It's much more than that because unless and until you recognize that you have, in your own power, in your mind, the capacity to acquire whatever you want from life, make life on your own terms—unless you acquire that—then you're not making the most of your potential ability.

Now this one trait is an important trait because due to this trait I was commissioned by Andrew Carnegie to give the world its first philosophy of individual achievement. This was the time that Mr. Carnegie and I started in 1908. Nobody had ever created a philosophy of success. It had never been done. Nobody had brought together all of the things that a man must do in order to succeed and make them into a philosophy. Now down through the years, we discovered these things that had to be done, and I found later on that when Mr. Carnegie chose me—I was a youngster then, only in my twenties—when he chose me in competition with men who were old enough to be my grandfather, many of them college professors. I was in competition with over 250 other people, and every one of them flunked the examination except myself. I would have flunked it if I hadn't had this trait, if he hadn't discovered there was potential in me. I hadn't developed it yet. I hadn't discovered it, but he knew it was there. I'm still giving you clues. Now you can change your first writing as I go along before I finally tell you what this one trait is. I'm satisfied that some of you will want to change. I give something pretty to read, your notes; after I have told you what it is. It's so simple. You're going to be surprised when I tell you what it is.

I went to see Mr. Carnegie to write a story about him. I was being paid $250 by a magazine to write a story. Little did I suspect that my interview with Mr. Carnegie would change, not only my whole destiny in life, but would through me change the destiny of millions of people, some of them not yet born. But that's the effect this had, and I got this wonderful assignment only because Mr. Carnegie had kept me there at his home three days and nights during which he was plying me with questions, looking inside of me and outside of me, and he finally came up with the idea that I had this one trait that he had been searching for that he didn't find in these other 250 people, all of whom were better educated. They were older than I and had a lot more ability in many ways, but they didn't have this one trait. They could've acquired it, but Mr. Carnegie came to the conclusion that not one of them had that temperament about them that would motivate them in acquiring this trait even though they knew how to do it.

Regardless of what you learn here in this, regardless of what you learn from Mr. Stone's marvelous guidance after you get out there in the field—and it's wonderful, I'll tell you that—if you don't have this one trait, you might as well turn in your book before you start because you'll not be a success. You'll not be a success in anything no matter what you choose in life unless you have this one trait, and it's the one thing that you and you alone control. I'm getting pretty hot now on all this. You don't control your wife or your husband. You may think you do, but you don't. You don't control your bank account. You may think you do, but you don't. You can get wiped out in a hurry. I ought to know. I've had experience. Matter of fact, when you look around, there's only one thing in this world that you control, and that's the thing that I'm talking to you about right now, and I have not yet told you what it is. And you've written down what you think it is.

When Mr. Carnegie got through talking to me for three days and nights, during which I had asked him a lot of questions and he'd asked me a lot, he said, "I've been talking to you now for approximately three days about a new philosophy, which I think somebody ought to create—a philosophy based upon the know-how of men like myself who have spent a lifetime finding out what to do and what not to do in order to succeed. You have heard from me all that I know about the potentials and the possibility of this philosophy. I've told you everything that I know about it. Now I want to ask you a question—just one question—and I want you to answer that question with a 'yes' or a 'no,' but don't answer it until you make up your mind which it is." I'm going to put the problem to you just as definitely as he put it to me. I'm going to ask you just as definitely after I get through talking whether or not you have this trait and, if you don't have it, whether or not you think you will develop it. Your answer there will depend on your future success, believe you me. He said, "If I commission you to become the author of the world's first philosophy of success, give you letters of introduction that'll open any door from the president of the United States on down and get the collaboration of hundreds of men whose help you'll need, if I do that, are you willing to devote 20 years of your life to research organizing this philosophy, paying your own way as you go along without any subsidy from me, yes or no?"

There I sat, with barely enough money in my pocket to pay my way back home, in front of the richest man in the world who had proposed to me to go to work for 20 years without compensation or without any subsidy. What would you have said? Yeah, that's just exactly what I tried to say. Just exactly. I could think of five or six reasons why I couldn't possibly afford to accept that assignment. In the first place, I wasn't quite sure what that word *philosophy* meant. In the second place, I didn't have any money to back me up for 20 years. In the third place, I didn't have enough confidence in Napoleon Hill to believe that I could carry out an assignment like that. That's three good reasons, and I could think of about three more. Isn't it strange how when we come up against problems—potential problems—we think of the "no can do" part of it and don't pay any attention to the "can do."

Isn't it wonderful how the mind works? Or is it wonderful? It's unfortunate, believe me, because we jump to the negative side always, not recognizing that oftentimes the greatest blessings that come to us in life come through our failures and our defeats and what we learn from them, what we learn about ourselves when we're up against a struggle and we go down in defeat. If we'll only remember this one thing: that every adversity, every failure that you meet will carry literally the seed of equivalent benefit if you'll begin to look for that seed. You'll find oftentimes that your failures are your greatest blessings.

Well, I sat there and rubbed my hands and the magazine I had opened, and I tried to open this big mouth of mine to tell Mr. Carnegie three or four reasons why I couldn't accept his offer. And then all of a sudden, I had a great light. I was curious as to why that great man had kept an unknown youngster like myself at his home for three days and nights. I was curious, and all of a sudden I got the answer. I said, "That man has discovered something in me that I didn't know was there, and it must be a very great something because he's offering me an opportunity, an opportunity such as I have never heard of being offered to any other man in my field. And I blurted out, I said, "Yes, Mr. Carnegie. You can not only depend upon me undertaking the mission, sir, but I will carry it out." He grabbed me by the hand and shook hands with me and said, "I not only like what you say, but I like the way you say it. I like the snap you put into it. I like the look in your eyes because I know you mean it." He said, "You didn't ask me any questions as to how you'd go about it. You probably didn't know and you probably didn't care. All you know is you're going to do the job. Is that right?" I said, "That's exactly right, Mr. Carnegie. Whenever I come up against problems, I always find solutions for those problems, and I guess there'll be plenty in these next 20 years."

What do you think he was searching for in me? What was he looking for? I want you to tell me. It would be far better if you tell me which it is than I tell you what it is. You know, a master sales-man tries to get the buyer to think he's doing the selling. If I can plant this idea in your mind, you come up with it, show me how smart you are—it'll remind me of what I had when I was a young-ster. My grandfather took me up to the barn. He raised chickens, special blooded chickens. He had hundreds, thousands of them maybe, and he'd scatter the grain all around over the ground, and then he'd cover it over with straw and hide it. "Well, Grand-father, what are you doing that for? Why don't you fix it so the chickens can find it?" He said, "Well now, I'll tell you, son. You won't understand this, but I have good reasons for hiding it. First place, I want to let the chickens feel how smart they are from scratching it out where I hid it for them, and in the second place, I want them to get the physical development in their bodies in the process of scratching it out."

What a grand thing it is if you can motivate a man to use his own ideas, to use his own thinking, and to come up with his own ideas, rather than to accept ready-made, handmade ideas of other people. I think one of the finest things about this science of success philosophy is it makes men resourceful. When you come up against a problem, you may not know the answer, but you find it before you're through. I'm giving you some red-hot clues.

What do you have written down on your paper? Honestly, what have you written down? What is this one trait that you've got to have before you can succeed at anything? Life is a complex thing. Nobody dodges problems—nobody. We all have them. But the amount of success that you enjoy in life will depend entirely upon how you relate yourself to problems. I'm not talking about your successes. I'm talking about your failures and your defeats. That's your determining factor—how you react when failure overtakes you, when opposition springs up in front of you. How you react then is going to be the determining factor. Now I'm getting very hot to this one trait—very hot. And you all know exactly what it is. If you're thinking as intensely as I think you are, you know exactly what it is.

Mr. Carnegie was looking for this one trait. He knew that during 20 years of research—and research is never profitable and always costly to the researcher—he knew the going would be hard, and he knew that I would time and time again have opportunity and invitation and motive for quitting. And we all run up against that. You'll find that you won't be in the field two days until you find a half dozen motives why you think maybe you've chosen the wrong thing. You'll find it. Sure you will, and your reaction when you make that discovery—your reaction is going to be the determining factor as to how successful you will be in this business or in any other business. Now, Mr. Carnegie knew that I would have problems. He knew I would run up against opposition, knew that the going would be hard. The 250 people that he examined also knew that, and they couldn't take it, and I could take it. How did it come that I could take it? He discovered that I had this one trait—that when the going is hard, instead of quitting, I turn on more steam and become determined that I'll not accept defeat at anything, except as a stepping stone to greater effort the next time. In other words, I had that particular temperament I guess in me inherently, although it took Mr. Carnegie to bring it out. I had that inherent quality, which causes defeat to have the same effect upon me that a red flag does upon a bull. Now you can get that one, can't you? You know, if you want to make friends with a bull, you go out with a red flag, and he really will make friends with you. And if you want to really find me a winner, you just put a hard problem before him, and you'll find out if he's a winner or not according to the way he attacks that problem or allows it to attack him. Every time you talk to anybody in this business that you're going into, there's going to be a stalemate. Do you know that? Every single time. Had you thought of it? Well, now the question is, who's going to make the sale? Are you going to buy a "yes," or is the other fellow going to buy a "yes" from you, or are you going to buy a "no" from him? That's the point—turning on more steam.

I'm going to close my talk, friends, with one illustration that will give you an idea of what I mean. During all these 20 years that I was doing research for Mr. Carnegie, I was making my living training salespeople. I've trained over 30,000 of them. I have trained more men in the life membership of the Million Dollar Roundtable and in the life underwriting field than any man living, probably. I expect that fully one-third of its total membership in the United States in the life membership of the Million Dollar Roundtable is there because of the influences that I gave them.

Now when I was training salespeople in New York many years ago, I came into my desk one morning a little bit late, and my secretary had put on my desk a little memorandum, and it said, "The President of the Newark Laundry Company says that he wishes you would come over to Newark and talk to him about training his sales organization. He's having some difficulty with his salesmen." I never heard of a laundry having salesmen. That was a new field to me, and it challenged me. And I said, "Well, I'm going to condition my mind before I go over to assure I make a sale even before I start over." And would you be interested in knowing how that could be done? You would?

You'd be interested in knowing how you make a sale before you go in to see a man? Let me get back a little further than that. Do you know to whom a sale is made before it is made to the man that puts his name on the dotted line? It's made to the salesman himself, isn't it? No matter what the fellow says, no matter what he looks like or what he says, you make up your mind before you get out of there that he's going to buy. Well, I went into my office. I closed my door, and I instructed my telephone operator not to connect my phone until I came out. I sat down at my desk, and I said, "Now you're going over to Newark, and you're going to talk to this man, and you're not coming back until you've made a sale. Now is that clear to the boy in here? You're not coming back until you make a sale. If you have to stay over there six months, you are going to stay over there until he'll buy in order to get rid of you. You're not coming back." And then to make sure when the psychological moment came, when I had auto-suggested myself even to the point where I was sure I would make a sale regardless of what he said, I called in my manager, who was managing these classes. I said, "Now Jack, you and I are going over to see the president of Newark Laundry Company. He wants to talk to us about training his salesmen. We're not coming back until we make a deal." He said, "How do you get that not coming back stuff? I have a wife and three kids." "Well", I said, "I have a wife and three kids, too. I'm coming back and so are you, but we are not coming back, my friend, until we make a sale. Now I want you to get that in your head before we start." I took him along for this reason. This was a man that I had trained over a long period of time at a goodly cost—a good many thousands of dollars—and I knew that if I fell down on at least one point, that I had been talking to my classes about so much, I'd ruin a good man. I wanted him there so that when this point came along and that laundry man showed signs of saying "no," I couldn't possibly weaken because my trusted assistant was right there watching. Big boss himself was on trial, and I had to make good. In other words, I was having myself trailed and supervised.

Well, we went over. It was a hot August day, the hottest day I've ever felt, and we got there, I guess, a little bit before noon. The man came out of his office and said, "Well, gentlemen, it's very warm. Let's go over to the Athletic Club. It's nice and cool over there. We'll have a nice lunch, and when the lunch is over, we'll go out into the library to sit down and talk this whole matter out. I thought to myself, "Boy, isn't that a good start?" I looked at Jack, and he winked at me: *Oh, this is just as much as in the bag*, and that's what he thought and that's what I thought—just like it was really in the bag. Well, we went over there, and during all of this luncheon this man was talking and telling me his troubles, and I was listening. By the time he got through talking, I didn't eat a bite. I was listening and building plans as I went along. When he got through, I knew exactly what to say to him. And we went out into the library.

"Now, Mr. Hill, the floor is yours," he said. I went ahead. I told him what I thought caused the trouble. I found out, by the way, that...he had a great army of drivers, and they were on a commission and salary basis. Most of their income was dependent upon the commission they got, and they had to hold on to their customers or they didn't get much commission. Something had developed that they were losing their business. I found out what that something was. I told him how it could be corrected. I told him how long it would take me to do the job. I told him how much it would cost. I gave him all the details, and he didn't bat an eye. I was watching his face very carefully to see if he squinted or changed his expression when I mentioned my fee, which is rather substantial. He says, "Okay." I could just see that he had bought my story. As I got down to almost the end, I slowed down a little bit. I came up for air for a few seconds. He said, "Well, Mr. Hill, I want to tell you I appreciate you boys coming over here. I like your story. I like you boys. I like you, and I like your efficiency. I think you can do a wonderful job." I looked over at Jack, and again he winked at me: *Boy, didn't we do a job there.* He said, "But..." Well, that *but* was like a rubber ball. It went up and hit the ceiling and came down and hit the floor, hit me in the eye and then hit Jack in the eye, only he didn't feel it. "When I called you, I telephoned two other men and gave them the same invitation that I gave you, and you just happened to get over here ahead of the other two. Now, we have an appointment with the other two for tomorrow, after which we will telephone you and let you know. I think you're going to get the job; don't misunderstand. I'm pretty sure you will, but tomorrow we'll let you know."

Now there was a good chance to pick up your hat. You see, he'd been a perfect gentleman. He had made it very easy for us. He bought us a nice lunch, only I hadn't eaten any of it. That was our place to bow ourselves out. All right, tomorrow. Remember my commitment: I said we're going over there and we're not coming back until we make a sale. I looked at Jack. He was sitting like this, and he got up about like that. He still had his hands on the round arms of the chair. I gave him a look that must've frozen him, too, because he dropped back down like that. If he had gotten out of that chair, if he had gotten on his feet to buy that "no," I'd have fired him the moment we got outside the man's office. And he was ready to do it. The man had given him a logical reason. He could see that there was no sale for the time being. But I didn't see that. I didn't go over there to buy a "no." I went over there to buy a "yes."

Now what would you have done at that point? You're going to come to that point, every one of you; you'll come to that very place where you can see...you pick up your little package and out you'll go. You're going to come to that point, and you're going to remember this story when you do. It's very easy to buy a "no." It's the easiest thing in the world, and the most natural thing that I know of for a beginner in the field. I have never seen a new salesman without training in my life that didn't buy a "no" easy— easier than anybody else in the world. He'd buy it because he's halfway expecting it. I don't want you to go out halfway expecting it. I want you to go out halfway expecting and more than halfway expecting that you're not going to buy a "no," that you're going to sell the man a "yes." What would you have done at that point?

Well, if you had been a hardened old customer in the sales field like I have been, you would have done just exactly what I did. I totally ignored everything he said, and I went into the second page of my sales talk. I said, "Well, Mr. X, I appreciate what you said, but now here is something that I didn't tell you about." And then I went into it. You see, I had some ammunition up my sleeve. If you go in and shoot your entire wad the first time, you're out. You need some rebuttals.

You know what a rebuttal is? If you want to sell, you better know what a rebuttal is. You better have a lot of them up your sleeve. Well, I went into my rebuttal. First presentation I consumed about 10 minutes. I had been going about five minutes, six minutes, seven minutes, and by that time, this man had his handkerchief out and was mopping his brow. I never have seen a man sweat as much as he did. I was really giving it to him. But my skin was just as dry as my skin is now. My collar wasn't even wet. I had conditioned myself mentally, spiritually, and physically not to accept anything except what I went after, and you can do that. I told him some things that I hadn't included in my first presentation, and when I slowed down a little bit, he said, "Now, Mr. Hill, I'm still with you, but what would you do if you were in my place?"

Now there was the shot I was waiting for. It was just the question I wanted him to ask me. What do you think I told him? What would you have told him? I said, "I know what I'd do if I were in your place. You know very well that I have the ability to do your job. You know that, don't you?" He said, "Yes, I do." I said, "I'd call those other two men and tell them that you've already employed a man." "Well that's an idea of how to do it... It's a deal." He started out, and I looked back, and Jack was still sitting there. I said, "Come on, Jack, let's go." We shook hands with the man and started down the street, and then I let down, first time, for two hours that I had let down in my attention, and when I did, the great beads of perspiration as big as any finger burst out all over me. I was wet as if I had swum in the East River, and in a little while, I just collapsed. I just collapsed right down on the sidewalk, and Jack said, "Oh he knocked at you hard, didn't he?" I said, "Not so much as I can't get up and tell you one thing, Jack. If you had gotten out of your chair, off of your fanny, when you were getting ready to do it, I would've fired you the moment we got out of there because you were getting ready to buy a 'no' and I was staying there to sell a 'yes.' I want you to remember from this example that you've had that it's the fellow that doesn't buy a 'no' that wins out in life, no matter what the circumstances are, how much they may seem to be against you. If you don't buy those circumstances—'they were just too bad; I couldn't do any-thing about it'—then you're more than apt to win out. "

I want you to learn a lesson from this. I have no way of know-ing what life holds for you. You have no way of knowing. It's just as well, I guess, that we don't. But regardless of how bright or how smart or how able you may be, you're going to run against circumstances that you will need to meet with all of your wits and all of your brains and all of your resources, and the one thing that you can do always, no matter how unthinkable the circumstance, the one thing that you can do is to say, "I don't know how I'm going to go around this one, but I'll tell you one thing—I'm never going to stop until I do go around."

What is the one thing to which Hill was referring—the one trait that you absolutely must have in order for any success principles to work? What is the one thing Napoleon Hill touted in this lecture as the trait that, if absent, will put a screeching halt to success each and every time? It is the determination to win. Your magic key will unlock your success only if you have a concentrated and unfaltering belief that it will work—so much so that you won't stop trying until you prove yourself right.

*Are you going to buy a "no" or sell a
"yes"? Have the determination to win!*

Acknowledgments

Successful people surround themselves with other successful people. Just like the saying—"your net worth is equal to your network." When we decided to write *Success and Something Greater: Your Magic Key*, we thought it would be a wonderful opportunity to invite people to join us on our journey. They had an opportunity not only to be present for many of the interviews, but to participate with their own questions and insightful reviews. We truly appreciate the following people, who stood up and said, "Count me in!" Thank you for your contributions to our interviews and your enthusiasm for Napoleon Hill and his Magic Key!

MEMBERS:

Ken Courtright

Kerri Courtright

Wade Danielson

Dr. Isaura Gonzalez

Dr. Emily Letran

Joan E Magill

Ricky Mendez

Jeanne O'Neale

Gregory Tatsch

Jeff Thompson

Associate:

Adam Kipnes

Sandra Kipnes

OUR FABULOUS TEAM:

Katrina Gains Thornton

Angela Totman